] *Co*

"*Counting Hope* is one of the most engrossing books I've ever read. It pulls you into a life that's full of love, conflict, triumph, and real consequence. It reads like a thriller, but one that gives you the tools to be a better person at home and at work. This isn't a dry classroom tutorial of new rules; it's the chance to virtually live another life beyond your own experiences. Emotionally powerful and at times jaw-dropping, I defy you to try and put it down once you've started."

—**George Fiscus**, Owner/Managing Partner

"Hope continues to speak with an authentic voice that allows all women to see themselves in her poetic words. Her courage to share her story is an inspiration to others who seek a clear path out of violence and addiction."

—**Marilyn Vetter**, Group Vice President, Government and Public Affairs

"Mueller's colorful journey is captured with such raw emotion, honesty, and openness. Rarely can you find so many life lessons in one place, from child-rearing to managing addiction, abuse, and escape. This book lent its emotional ride of discovery to how our younger years impact our lives and future careers. Mueller manages to fuel her drive and goal-oriented attitude by the darkness of her past; such a tale of perseverance and the uncovering of self-worth."

—**Amy Margeson**, Vice President ISO & Regulatory

"Wow! What a wild ride of a read. Again, Hope has beautifully and hauntingly captured the human spirit in times of turmoil and triumph. I can feel the pain, apprehension, angst, and joy jumping off the pages. Hope Mueller has a gift for relaying and vividly painting scenarios that bring the reader right along as if we're right there with her."

—**Jennifer Hottell**, Community Engagement Director

"A gripping, sometimes brutal, but ultimately empowering read. Mueller is unflinching as she takes us on a roller-coaster ride of domestic abuse and addiction interspersed with amazing personal and professional success stories. Her account is alternately heavy then uplifting, raw then inspiring. *Counting Hope* is required reading for anyone who has ever felt trapped in a bad situation or struggled to overcome past mistakes. Mueller proves that once you truly believe in your own worth, anything is possible."

—**Jennifer Bushey**, Technical Specialist

"Three words: perseverance, perseverance, perseverance. Hope Mueller shares a story that is both horrifying and inspiring. The reader is there with her through her trauma and her joys. Hope follows a path to joy with the first steps taken by her success at work. Step by step, she claws her way to triumph. Once you start reading, you won't be able to put it down, then you will want to read it again to make sure you did not miss anything. The reader is left reflective, inspired, and ultimately shares in Hope's current happiness."

—**Susan Chambers**, Senior Housing Manager

"Hope tells the raw and compelling story of her liberation from abuse and taking control of her own destiny. She directs her narrative to the reader, who in all too many lives is hopelessly trapped in a downward spiralling tragedy. Her lessons learned are ours in escaping the culture of death."

—Colonel Dick Mueller

"*Counting Hope* is an eloquent account of one woman's journey to adulthood. The author pulls no punches when sharing the gritty, tumultuous circumstances of her past. Hope's memoir takes us from her unconventional high school years to a final, devastating family loss. The reader is engaged in her path to healing and self-discovery. The book inspired me to be accountable for decisions made, accurately reflect on my role in life, and dream big for the future. No one's life is always easy, but *Counting Hope* reminds you to imagine the ultimate future."

—Jennifer Harp, Owner/Operator, Leahy's Greenhouse

"I loved every detail of *Counting Hope*. Hope keeps the reader so engrossed with every word. I felt present in her life story as she led us through the trials and tribulations. Very well written with intense emotion and detail that had me in tears of happiness and tears of sadness as Hope fought her way to a better life for herself and her children. She has succeeded in more ways than one. Inspirational, to say the least."

—Kristie White-Scott, Supernova

"Make sure your schedule is clear because you won't want to put down *Counting Hope: From Conflict to Confidence*! This is a touching and, at the same time, gripping story of how a woman overcomes significant and heartbreaking challenges as a wife, mother, daughter, and rising professional."

—**Melanie Neal**, Vice President Commercial Operations

"Hope's honest portrayal of a dysfunctional marriage riddled with drug addiction and coupled with physical and emotional abuse is candid and haunting. There were parts I had to put down, as well as those I couldn't stop reading. The psychological trauma she endures is overshadowed only by the hope that dawns within her and slowly grows to a climax as she discovers her worth as a woman, worker, mother, and wife. Hope's writing is true and raw and mesmerizing."

—**Beth Lottig**, Publisher

counting hope

hope mueller

Hunter Street
PRESS

Published by Hunter Street Press

ISBN: 978-1-950685-27-1 paperback
ISBN: 978-1-950685-28-8 hardcover
ISBN: 978-1-950685-29-5 ebook

Library of Congress: 2020908117

Printed in the United States

CONTENTS

DEDICATION

To Ashlei and Olivia, thank you for letting me tell this story. To my husband, Brad, this book would not be possible without you. To Brooke and Lauren, thank you for honoring my writing time. To anyone who needs to hear this, know when it is time to get out.

PREFACE

The material in this book is the truth, as I know it, as I experienced it through my eyes. I know that each of us has our own perception of the truth. I recognize that other people's memories of the events may be different than my own. The book was not intended to harm anyone, hurt anyone's feelings, or portray them negatively. Everyone involved in the publication, marketing, and support of this book all confirm there is no intention of harm, hurt, or disparagement.

I have changed names, made tweaks to settings and description, to allow people to remain anonymous. To the best of my ability, I have remained honest to my perception of the truth.

This is a continuation of my story after the completion of *Hopey: From Commune to Corner Office*. This book stands on its own, and reading *Hopey* is not required to understand the events unfolding in this work.

This book is graphic and intense, includes extreme language, violence, drug use, sex, death, and healthcare procedures.

ASHLEI'S SNAPSHOT

*P*ing.

The elevator doors slide open. An antiseptic scent bounces off gleaming white walls. My fiancé, Tom, holds my hand, and I cling to his. I am girding for a nightmare.

Mom must have heard the elevator. She is the first person I see. Her eyes. Her eyes. *What is she saying? Why does she look like that?*

"Hi, Mom," I muffle into her shoulder as she surrounds me, holds me, squeezes tight. I can feel the tension in her back, the tightness of her breath. "Where is Olivia?"

Tom waits by my side. "Hi, Hope," he says. Now it's his turn to be embraced so radically. Olivia joins us. We hug. She starts to cry.

"Ashlei, I'm sorry. I'm so sorry. I did everything I could."

"Olivia . . . where is Dad? Are you okay? Where is he? Where's Dad?"

I look at Mom. "Can I see him?"

"Yes, of course." Mom's moves are jerky. She is twisted up and forcing herself to breathe.

Olivia's fifteen-year-old face is puffy and looks aged. Her eyes hold a deeper despair than Mom's. She takes my hand. "I'll go with you. Don't leave me, Ashlei."

"Okay, baby, okay." I glance back at Tom. He gives me an encouraging nod.

I let Olivia lead me. She pushes the big button on the wall, and one heavy double door swings inward to the critical care unit. Mom is trailing us. Watching.

Beeps. Whooshes. More beeps. Tapping of fingers on keyboards. The clean scent is stronger here. It is a scene from a movie. *Is this real?* A tall, capable-looking nurse in blue scrubs approaches us.

"Hi," she smiles. The smile does not reach her eyes. Her eyes have the same haunted look. *What? What is it? Why does everyone look like that?*

Mom had told me it was bad, that Olivia was right, that I had to come. Now I have seen three people with this stare. *What? What does it mean? I can handle it, I swear.*

When Olivia called, she was hysterical and said the paramedics had taken Dad in an ambulance. She was left at a stranger's house and didn't know where she was. She was out of her mind. I couldn't calm her down or understand what she was saying. Her sucking sobs garbled her words. She couldn't tell me who was with her. Her hiccupping wails pierced through the phone. I tried to calm her down. I told her to breathe. I asked her if she had called mom yet. A tiny 'no' emerged through the broadband. I convinced her to call mom, even though she was worried mom would be mad at dad. She had to call mom. Mom would know what to do. Mom would to tell me if I needed to worry.

Mom was three hours away when she got Olivia's call. She took the next exit and headed south toward Bloomington. Someone needed to figure out what had happened. It was bad. Mom told me I had to come.

After the call from mom, I stood frozen, staring at my closet. I couldn't decide. *What do I take? What should I wear? What if there is a funeral?* I packed everything. Maybe all the stuff could hold me to the ground. Maybe the clothes could keep me on earth.

Now Olivia is leading me to Dad's room. But the nurse. The nurse's eyes look like Mom's. Olivia's are worse. Filled with more . . . *more what? More something.* An emotion? A truth I don't understand? I have never seen this look before, a mixture of sadness, empathy, and knowing. It is the knowing that scares me.

"You must be Ashlei." The nurse knows me. Knows my name.

I bob my head with a plastic smile. My face is stone. Time stops. The scene slows. The noise dulls. The beeps die out. My stomach roils.

"You are here to see your dad," the nurse says. Olivia is crushing my hand so hard it aches and starts to pierce the fog in my brain.

"Yes. Can I see him?"

"Of course. You will need to put these on." She hands me a yellow smock and a blue face mask. Olivia reaches for her own.

We turn to our right, and he is there. A million tubes. A million bags. Dad is motionless except his chest rising and falling from the air pushing through a hose snaking down his throat. I slide my eyes across five monitors. The closest one to me has ten flat lines marching across it.

Tears flood my eyes. I go to his side and take his hand. His hand is warm. I sit on a stool. Olivia stands behind me, quietly crying. She has someone to share her grief with; I'm here. Her sister.

"Daddy, Daddy, please wake up." I put my head to his hand and plead. Beg.

I feel Olivia's body shaking behind me, and I turn around and sob into her waist, into her belly.

I spin back and whimper into Dad's warm hand, mouthing the words on his skin. "Daddy, please . . . please wake up."

We are like that forever, for no time, for always. Maybe we are still there. The pain does not stop. We are a well of despair. The dark, cold water threatens to consume. To bury. *Where is my dad? Did he fall into this well? Is he here too?*

"Daddy, you have to wake up. You have to wake up. Please, Daddy, please . . ."

LOCKED IN

I thought I was running from my upbringing and what my mom was, when, in fact, I was racing headlong into the same life. When I moved out on my own at age fifteen, I recreated both the environs and the behaviors of the commune. There was no ownership of goods, we shared everything, we had beds on the floor, and there was too much pot smoking. The one thing we didn't do that I had seen as a kid in the commune was the swapping of sex partners. Thankfully my roommates, Katy, Jamaica, Susan, and I weren't into that.

By the time I moved in with my next roommate, Jennifer, I had started to leave those activities behind and grow up—or so I thought. Jennifer was a social and behavioral guide for me. We were two sixteen-year-olds living on our own, yet our apartment was normal enough. We each had our own room. Jennifer had a real bed. My mattress was still on the floor. I did not realize bed frames were normal and cheap. I never had a bedframe or headboard growing up. They seemed fancy and expensive to me, and totally unnecessary. My room was organized, as was the rest of the apartment. Jen and I were responsible, we both worked, went to school (we were juniors then seniors in high school), and we managed our lives well.

Jennifer was well trained in the home arts. She cooked, sewed, and had been an active 4-H'er. She even sewed her own prom dress our senior year. It was gorgeous. She cooked and shared with me her knowledge around the kitchen. At the holidays, Jennifer and her mom made candy for friends and family. She taught me how to make turtles and peanut butter balls. This is a tradition my family holds onto today. We have made candy every year, and my girls look forward to the joys of spending the day together and the fruits of our labor—or, more accurately, the *sweets* of our labor.

Other than almost blinding myself while scouring the shower with a sulfuric-acid-based bathroom cleaner, the year and a half in the apartment with Jen was steady and reliable. Those were not the terms I was raised by. It was the first time in many years that my life was not wild and unpredictable. I give Jennifer lots of credit for showing me how to create normalcy in life.

When new neighbors moved in below us, things changed. One morning I got out of the shower to someone pounding on the front door. With a towel wrapped around me and my hair in a swoop, I peered through the eyehole to see two police officers.

"Hello?" I cracked the door with the chain in place.

"Ma'am. We've had a complaint; could we talk to you?"

I shut the door enough to slide the chain off. My heart thumping in my chest, I wondered what had happened.

"We've had a report of loud music from this apartment."

"Ummm . . ." Confused, I looked behind me for some unseen and unheard answer. It was 6:20 in the morning, a school day. There was no noise from Jennifer's room. Our place was quiet. "My alarm went off at six. I have been in the shower." This was obvious with the towel ensemble.

"Do you have a roommate?"

"Yeah. She doesn't make any noise though." I looked around again at the noiseless place trying to think of a reason for any complaint. "Maybe it was my alarm?"

"No, the report said loud music was coming from this apartment all morning." The officers did not ask to come in, and I did not offer. I stood there, left hand on the door handle and right hand across my chest, making sure the towel stayed up and tucked in.

"I don't know what they heard. My alarm went off, and I pushed snooze a few times. No music has been playing." I responded with a shrug.

"Well, we don't hear or see anything suspicious. We will

leave you to your morning and talk to the complainant. Thank you, ma'am."

"Okay, sorry." *What am I sorry for?* "Have a good day," I mumbled as I shut them out. *And do I really look like a "ma'am"?*

Jennifer peered from her room in her pajamas. "Who was that?"

"The police. A neighbor complained that we had loud music playing."

"What?" she asked, her inflection high. "This morning? Now?"

"Yup." I unfurled the hair towel and started to rub my hair dry. I had to get ready for school.

It was the beginning of the end of our apartment. The neighbor called the police frequently with noise complaints. Jen and I tried to talk to them about it. An odd pair, an elderly mom and a middle-aged son, they wouldn't speak to us. They repeatedly banged on their ceiling with some implement, to let us know we were loud (which we rarely were), but they would not answer their door to us when we attempted to make peace. The cops checked in on us regularly, and it was always quiet. Exasperated by their constant complaints, when the neighbors banged on their ceiling, we began to stomp and jump around the apartment, clanging pans and causing a racket, because it did not matter if we were quiet or not; they were going to call the cops. And we were teenagers, after all.

The police showed up at least twice a week to tell us to turn down our non-existent music, but they never questioned us. Neither of us were eighteen, we were occasional pot smokers, and our names were not on the lease—Jennifer's parents were—so we considered ourselves lucky they didn't press us with more questions. One afternoon, the neighbor dude came up and yelled at Jennifer for a loud TV, when the TV wasn't even on. I heard him yelling at her, and I came out of my room to see what was happening. Jennifer was so upset; I slammed the door in his face. And he stood outside and yelled some more. I would not let him treat gentle Jennifer that way. Later that afternoon, we decided to move out.

We were on the tail end of our senior year of high school. Jen and I had both gotten into Indiana University, so being near campus made sense. We had steady boyfriends and thought it would be fun to move in together. All four of us signed the lease for a house on University Street, a mile from campus.

Our new place boasted hardwood floors, a tiny kitchen, three bedrooms, and an unfinished basement where we could hang out. Jennifer and I rented a huge belt sander, and the two of us refinished the hardwood floors in the entire house. This should have been our first sign about the boys who were moving in with us. The sander was huge and heavy, and we spent days sanding, then staining and coating, the floors—with little to no help from our boyfriends.

The house was great. Living with Jennifer was stable. We kept the place clean, mostly, and maintained a predictable and nice home. The boys never seemed to do their part. Jen's boyfriend, Frank, did not pay his rent on time, smoked pot, was not clean, and was a total asshole. Val, my guy, was the complete opposite. Val was a straight-laced rule follower. He did not like getting high, and he did not want me to do it either. Val worked out, studied, and wanted things a certain way. I gravitated toward order and followed suit, doing his bidding, and tried to make sure he was happy and satisfied. Val was controlling and expected me to obey. I was willing to oblige.

I worked at Frisch's Big Boy diner, a waitress and shift manager at age seventeen. The college kids under my watch hated me. I didn't let them leave until their side-work was finished, and I checked it before they were allowed to clock out. Jeez, I had to be freaking annoying. I was young, bossy, and probably came off as a know-it-all. It was my first leadership experience, at work at least, and it allowed me to earn extra money being shift manager. I took the job seriously and ensured the staff took care of the customers and the restaurant. When it came to work, I set goals and high standards for myself early on. But in relationships, that was another matter.

Val showed up unexpectedly while I was working at Frisch's one afternoon. He walked in the front door and demanded to see me. I told the other waitress I was going on my break, my smile fading as I studied the anger in Val's face.

What is he mad about? Shit. What did I do? I racked my brain for recent events. I hadn't gone out with my girl-friends. Our room was in order, the rent paid, I was work-ing, and classes were going well. I got all A's and one B my first full semester of college. *Why is he mad?*

"Hey," I started off with a big grin, trying to de-escalate whatever was going on. "What's up?"

"Let's go outside."

"Um, okay." I untied my apron, folded it neatly and looped the strings around it, following Val to his car. He slammed his door, rattling the little convertible. I raised my eyebrows in question.

"What's up?" I asked again, my voice high and tight.

"I am." He glared at me. "Do you have something to tell me?"

My heart and mind were speeding. He'd never been this mad before. Sure, we fought; it had never been physical, and usually he was pretty laid back. He was controlling, but he wasn't a loud yelling guy. I followed his rules, and I was on the straight and narrow—class, work, homework, repeat. I could not think of anything I did wrong.

"Um, no?" I tilted my head in question. "What's going on? What's wrong?"

"You know what you did. You knew it would make me mad."

"I honestly don't know what you're talking about. What's wrong?"

"What did you do last week? Did you go anywhere with Katy?" Val stared ahead, not looking at me, which ratcheted up the fear.

I thought through the previous week. *What did I do? Did we go anywhere?* Nothing. Nothing came to mind.

"No." Tears started to well up. "I went to class. I worked, and I picked up the extra shift on Saturday. I didn't do anything with Katy." I was crying now.

"Well, I know you and Katy smoked pot with Frank last week."

"No." I shook my head. "I did not. And I haven't seen Katy in weeks."

"Frank told me," he looked out the front window at the grey sky. "I don't want to be with you if you are going to smoke. We've talked about this."

No, no, no, no. I did not want to break up. I loved Val, or thought I did. Life was good. Patterned, predictable. I did what he said, but we were good, solid. I balled up in the small passenger seat, shocked we were having this conversation.

"No! We can't break up! I didn't do anything."

"Frank told me you smoked last week while I was in class. He told me you lie about not getting high anymore. He says you do it all the time."

"No! That's not true. Why would he tell you that? Why would you believe him over me?" I searched his face for understanding. "You know he is a liar. He doesn't pay his rent, doesn't go to class, doesn't work. He is a dick. Why would you believe anything he says?"

Shit, we even had a lock on the outside of our bedroom door to keep Frank out. Frank was stealing money from our change jar, and any money we left around disappeared. The bedroom doors did not have locks, so Val installed a hasp and a combo lock. We kept our room locked when we went out.

"I don't trust Frank. I don't trust Katy either." Val scowled at me. "And I don't trust you when you are with Katy."

"Val, look, I didn't do anything. I don't do anything with Katy anymore. I want to be with you. I don't want to break up!" I pleaded. "Why would I get high? I know you would be mad if I smoked. Why would I do it?"

I breathed in and tried to slow down my nerves. I was upset, and I needed to get back to work. We had fought in the car for longer than my break time. I didn't know why Frank lied to him, or why Val believed it.

"Why would Frank tell you that?" I asked again.

"Well, he and I were getting high after class today. Maybe since I was smoking, he thought he could share what you guys did last week."

I exhaled long and slow. There it was. Val could get high, do whatever, but I couldn't. More importantly, I didn't. I honestly did not care if Val smoked, and I couldn't spend any more time fighting in the parking lot. And the new information, that Val had smoked with Frank, shot strength into me.

"I don't like it that you are this upset over a lie. I have to go back to work." I patted down my hair and rubbed my face. "I don't want to break up over a lie."

"Yeah." Val appeared to be reconsidering his anger. He gave a slight nod.

"I love you." I swung open my car door. "See you when I get home."

I walked back to the restaurant, putting on my apron. I snuck into the bathroom to look in the mirror. My face was blotchy, and my eyes were red-rimmed. My reflection looked sad and confused. *Who is this person in the mirror? Who is she? And what the hell just happened?*

The parking lot fight started a string of escalating events. Val and I began to argue more and more. I never knew why he was so angry. One weekend I helped his mom wallpaper her bathroom, and she talked about her marriage and how Val's dad was dominant and dictatorial. He was easily angered, and she was always trying to adjust so he would not be mad. She lamented that she had to "dance" to her husband's desires. Whatever he wanted, she did. He got upset, and she would jump through hoops to try to make him happy. She told me it was oppressive and she wished she could break free, but once you have kids (she had five, four still at home), it's hard to see yourself out.

Val's mom warned me. She warned me in that bathroom, with the green-flocked wallpaper, that I did not have to do what Val wanted. She told me I was young and capable and I did not have to live my life following the whims of her son. I listened. *But did I hear her?*

The frequency of arguing with Val and the threats increased. The fights were almost physical, lots of shouting, and near pushing. We were going to break up every other day. But I stayed. We were both on the lease, sharing a room. If I moved out, I would still have to pay my portion of the rent while trying to cover expenses at a new place. It would be hard to do this on my waitress pay. I was behaving, trying to do everything right, and it wasn't good enough. I went to class. Got good grades. Worked full time. I did not smoke. A final blow up occurred in early May.

We fought about god knows what. I slammed the door

to our room and swore I was leaving. I shoved some clothes into my backpack. Yelling about what an asshole he was, I proclaimed I wasn't going to "dance" for him anymore. I didn't care that I had to pay rent; I was going to move out. My bag packed, I pulled hard on the door handle. It shook but did not budge. I tried the door again.

I was locked in.

Val had locked me in our room with the padlock.

I pummeled on the door. "Let me out! Open this door!"

No response.

"Hey, fucker, let me out of here!" I rattled the door some more. My brain raced through options. No way could I open the door from the inside. Our room had two windows. One led into a shed attached to the house, and one went directly into the front yard.

"Are you going to let me out? You can't keep me in here forever!"

Still nothing from outside of the door. *Did Val leave?* No, I could feel he was standing out there.

I punched in Susan's number on the phone next to our bed.

"Hey, Hopey, what's up?" she answered right away. Thankfully she was quick.

"Val locked me in the bedroom. I need you to come pick me up." I did not have a car. I walked everywhere or borrowed Jenny's car.

"What? What do you mean he locked you in your room?"

"You know the lock we put on the door because Frank was taking stuff from us? That. He locked it." I looked around, and a pool of sunlight languished on the smooth hardwood floor. This beam of light somehow gave me hope. "We were fighting. I was packing a bag to leave, and he locked me in here."

"Oh no, he didn't. I'm gonna kill that motherfucker!"

Gotta love Susan.

"Don't worry about it. Just come and get me!"

"Oh, hell yes! On my way!"

"Okay, I'm gonna jump out of the window."

"Wait! What?" Susan shrilled. "What?!"

"Susan, you know it's the first floor." I opened the window and judged the distance to the ground. "Maybe six feet. I've got this."

"Okay, I'm on my way."

I hung up the phone. Val must have heard some of the call or heard the window open.

"Hey, Hope," his voice came through the door. "You calmed down? You ready to talk?"

No response.

"Hey! You can't leave. You can't go anywhere. Talk to me. Let's talk."

I stayed quiet and tried not to make a noise. He knew I was in there.

"Do you want me to unlock the door?" Val asked.

"Fuck you! Leave me alone."

"Okay. I see you haven't calmed down. I will let you hang out in there a little longer." His feet shuffled away from the door.

I glanced around the room. *What else should I take?* I would have to come back and pack up my stuff at some point. What else did I need for the next few days? Nothing. I had my wallet and some clothes. I jammed my arm through the sling of the backpack and jostled it to center. I opened the window wide. Gripping the sill with both hands, I got my left foot secure on the opening. I heard metallic scrapes against the door. Val was taking off the padlock and coming in.

"Hey, what are you doing?" Val bellowed.

I looked back and lifted my right foot onto the sill and jumped. It was not far, but it was a rush. My adrenaline was high from the fighting, the fear of being imprisoned, and not being allowed to move about, even for the small amount of time. The outside felt fresh, bright, and new. Freedom.

"Hope! Where are you going?" Val yelled at me as his face popped through the open pane. "I was going to let you out."

"Well, you don't have to now. I got myself out," I shouted over my shoulder.

"Come back here! We need to talk."

I turned and jogged to the street, to where Susan would round the corner to scoop me up. I did not want Val coming out the front door. I did not want to talk anymore. I wanted out. I wanted to leave.

And I did.

One might think I realized I deserved to be treated better, and I did in that moment. But I was headstrong, young, and I rushed into the next disaster I created for myself. And it would be so much worse than Val could have ever been.

THREE WEEKS

"Shit!" The joint fell on my lap, narrowly missing the space between the seat and the console, where things get lost forever. "Shit!" I giggled and picked up the fatty before it burned my leg or the seat. Katy's 1983 Honda Civic had seen worse. There were more than a few burn marks. We had covered the car with stickers and figurines to make up for the damage.

"Wait, Hope," Katy glanced in her review mirror. "Wait."

"What?" I peered around to see what she was looking at. I didn't see a cop, so I lifted the joint to my lips and inhaled.

"Who is that behind us?" Katy asked. "They've been following us for a couple of blocks. And he is riding my ass."

"Hmmm, I don't know. Here." I handed her back the shrinking blunt. I unrolled the window to let some of the dense smoke free. I waved my hand to clear the car.

"Well, if it was a cop, I guess they would have pulled us over by now." Katy took her turn sucking on the joint.

The silver car trailed close behind. I looked back. "He sorta looks familiar. Is it Frank?"

"No . . ." With a flash of recognition, Katy said, "I know who it is. It's Matt."

The car behind flashed its lights.

"What does he want?"

"Fuck if I know."

"You think he saw us getting high?"

"Yeah, probably."

Katy turned into a nearby parking lot. I shoved the joint into the tiny ashtray and pushed it closed. *Hopefully the whole roach won't burn out, and we can smoke it later.*

Matt pulled in behind us.

"Let's see what he wants," Katy said, as she swung open her door. We rambled out of the car. I leaned against the door, while Katy sashayed to the back where he was walking toward her.

"Hey, Matt. What's up?"

"Hey, Katy. What are you guys doing?" he smirked.

"Nothing. Just driving around. You?"

"It looks like maybe you were smoking?"

"Huh?" She shot a look at me. *What should she say?*

I gave her the slightest shoulder shrug. I did not know this guy, never met him.

"This is Hope." She nodded in my direction. I raised my hand and grinned.

"Hey, Hope." He gave a half wave and looked at Katy. "Were you guys getting high?"

She rolled her eyes at him.

"Can I have some?" Matt asked. "If you're not doing anything, let's go to the park and you can share."

"Oh!" Katy laughed off her nervousness and checked my response. I gave another shrug. Katy laughed again. "Jesus, Matt, if you knew we were smoking, you didn't think following me so close and flashing your lights at us would freak me the fuck out?"

"Ha! Sorry. I wanted to join you."

"All right," Katy agreed. "Let's go to my house."

I folded back into the seat and shut the door.

"Yeah, that's Matt."

I didn't know it then, but I would spend the next eleven years of my life with the guy I had just met.

We got high at Katy's house. She left to go to work, so Matt and I drove around for the rest of the afternoon. It was midsummer, I was not back to class yet, and I wanted to play. After I'd climbed out of the window and left Val, I stayed at my mom's for a few weeks then moved into an apartment on Olive Street. Matt dropped me off there later that day, and we hung out every day after.

Matt was a carpenter, and a few years older than

me—five to be exact. He was living at his mom's house in between apartments, or at least that was the story he told me at the time. In retrospect, I should have asked more questions.

I was eighteen, would turn nineteen in August, the first summer after freshman year, still working as a waitress at the Big Boy and taking on extra hours at a daycare. Life was pretty good. I was not looking for anything serious. I was not looking for anything specific at all. Recently free from Val, I wanted to be carefree. That didn't happen.

About a week later, on our first official date, Matt told me what he wanted me to wear. He reminded me to put on makeup, which I usually didn't do. I should have taken this as a sign, but in truth I liked it, it was comfortable. I liked the directness. I liked the control and strength. I liked the order and structure being with strong men demanded from me. Matt knew what he wanted, and I wanted to be that for him. I knew I could. Maybe it was some warped way of me proving to myself how capable I was. At school I was able to please my teachers, male and female, with my hard work. Maybe the people pleaser in me thought it was the same thing with a male partner.

Matt and I settled into a routine. He got up early, donned his carpenter gear—worn-out jeans, work boots, leather belt, and hammer holder—and went to work. I thought it was sexy. Since Val was no longer in my life telling me not to get high, I did. I smoked a lot. I was untamed. Although I went to school and worked, I spent plenty of time getting high with friends, mountain bike riding, exploring, and doing mini-adventures with my fellow pot-smokers.

In August, right before school started, Matt and I watched *The Doors* movie starring Val Kilmer as Jim Morrison and Meg Ryan as his girlfriend, Pam. Pam and Jim were wild and in tune with each other. They were stormy and intense. I loved it. The movie inspired feral passion.

After the movie, Matt and I took off in the night. We ran in the dark, riotous and free. We went to the park, paced the one-mile running trail, then circled the bases on one of the softball fields. It was exhilarating to run! The inky night was heavy on our bodies. We climbed onto the roof of a shelter house and laid back to look at the stars. We talked about the world, our universe, and our nothingness. Resting didn't last long. We clambered down, explored the thin creek, and scaled the bridge. Then we ran some more. Fully in our bodies, as little thought as possible, we were physical beings alight with the stars. White bright lights bouncing on the globe. Tracing our energy through the black curtain of night.

We raced up the street to the playground. I looked back at Matt; I was winning, running faster. Matt looked surprised at my speed and stamina. His eyes were bright. Curious. I was a spectacle to him. I could read it on his face.

What fairy had he caught? Who was this girl who wanted to run in the dark and showed no fear? His thoughts played on his face a picture of wonder, desire, and excitement. We charged the playground equipment like an obstacle course, pushing ourselves hard. As we jogged back to the apartment, we laughed. The blackness hugged us, and we breathed hard as a sheen of sweat glinted off of our bare arms. A raw feeling coursed through me—it was unabashed joy.

And it was not to last.

The next day started again with the early rise and Matt trudging off to work. I made my bed, as always, which now had a bedframe. My bedspread was pink, and I still had the oak desk Mom and I reclaimed from the trash heap and refinished. I liked my room. I liked my life. Matt had essentially moved in. He stayed over every night, had a small clutch of clothes in the closet, but we never talked about being boyfriend and girlfriend. We did not talk about "our relationship"—we slipped into it. Maybe all young relationships are this way? It was not an agreement, a discussion; it just was. He was hanging out at my house. All I wanted was to play.

One evening Matt sat on the bed, and I sat at the desk smiling at him. I relished a moment of happiness. I felt full joy, with a touch of silliness. I was high.

"I feel so pink!" I blurted out, giggling.

"What? You feel what?" Matt questioned.

"Ha!" I smiled back and laughed into the word. "Pink!"

"Girl, you are crazy . . ." he mumbled, taking another toke off of the roach we were nursing.

My sophomore year of college started, and I returned to studying and working full time. Classes were getting harder; molecular biology and organic chemistry filled my days. I had a small study group, each premed like myself. A trio of fellow students, Jon, Nancy, and Tracy, rounded out my study crew. Jon was from a family of doctors; Nancy was a refined lily-white girl, small and quiet; and Tracy was a Hooters waitress and a bit grungy like me. I am not sure how we all teamed up, but it did seem to work. One afternoon Tracy and I were at her place, smoking a joint and studying. She complained about how hard organic chemistry was, how she was worried she was going to fail. It did not dawn on me at the time that getting high while studying could perhaps be a problem. Tracy cracked open the book and started reading. I looked at her, appalled.

"What are you doing?"

"What do you mean? I'm reading this chapter."

"You can't read the chapter!" I shouted.

"What? How else are you going to study the material?"

"Fuck, girl, that is your problem," I pontificated. "You can't *read* organic chemistry. Is that how you've been studying?"

"Yeah." Her face was stuck between frustration and curiosity, her brow knitted.

"You can't read it! You have to *do* it! You have to work the problems." I whipped open my notes from class. "The test will be on the problems from class. Did you take notes?"

"Yeah, I write down everything he does."

"Good, get those out. Organic is like math or physics. We work the problems, do them over and over again, and we use the book if we are stuck or don't get the problem."

I felt like a natural-born teacher. It seemed obvious to me how to study. "Try the first equation he showed us in class today."

Shit, no one can read an entire organic chemistry chapter; well, no one I have ever met. It's as boring as hell. With organic chemistry, you have to jump in and do the work. Just like life.

Tracy got the hang of it, and it felt good to help her understand the material. It felt good to feel smart, to be a mentor, and to set goals for good grades. My grades were great, and I had developed good study habits, or maybe it was an innate ability to focus. I worked full time, got high with friends, even during study sessions, and I did okay. Not just okay, pretty damn well. *What could I have been if I was not smoking weed? What could I have accomplished if I was not stoned?*

Christmas passed, and the second semester of my

sophomore year started with the same mix of work and school and studying. Time to refill my birth control pills, I went to Planned Parenthood as always, but I was due for a mandatory annual exam. I had to make an appointment to come back, so I grabbed a handful of condoms from the dish on the counter to tide me over until my exam in three weeks.

I did not think much of it, which was a recurring theme during this time—not thinking. I was living life, going to school, working, hanging out with friends, and having fun with Matt. We were having fun. We were not in love. It was nothing. It was convenient. It just was. Tossing Matt the condoms, I told him we would get the pills in three weeks, so we had to be careful for a while. We weren't concerned about getting pregnant. I mean, intellectually I knew I could. I was of age. I was a healthy young lady with a regular period. I also thought three weeks was nothing, and there was no way I could get pregnant in three weeks. I had been on the pill for a few years, and there must be some residual effects, right? Why I thought this I have no idea. A stellar student, I was premed, but I was also stupid.

Three weeks later, I went in for the exam. I was handed a cup for a urine sample. The nurse pointed to the bathroom I had been to several times before. I left my sample in the stainless steel pass-through, washed up, and settled into the narrow waiting room chair. The faded teal green chairs had seen many patients, all here for affordable healthcare and sometimes an abortion. In our Bloomington clinic, abortions were done on Thursdays. *Why do I know that? How do I know that?* I looked around and knew none of these people were here for an abortion because today was Friday. I snatched the newspaper resting on the small table next to me and flipped through the pages.

"Hope?"

"Hi." I got up and followed the nurse to a small room, which was not an exam room. There was no table with a paper cover, no stirrups. It was a closet converted into an office.

"Take a seat."

"Um, okay. I'm here for my annual."

"Yes. We won't be able to do the exam today."

Confused, I sat down. Pamphlets were scattered over the round tabletop. I debated stacking them neatly.

"Wait here. A counselor will be in shortly." She swooshed the door open, and it softly closed behind her.

Well, if we can't do the exam today, I will reschedule. I need to get to class. I hope they will give me the script until I can get in for another appointment. Maybe they had an emergency, and they can't do any exams? I resisted ordering the brochures, their disarray bothering me, and I was starting to get antsy. *Why can't they do the exam?*

I stood up, deciding I did not need to wait. I would

reschedule the appointment. I put my hand on the door handle, and it swung open, and I almost fell onto a short blonde woman.

"Oh!"

"Oh! Ha! I'm sorry," I apologized for the near collision.

"That's okay." She stepped into the room, and I moved back. The door closed itself. "Have a seat."

"I can reschedule the appointment since we can't do it today."

"Oh. No. Have a seat, please." She gestured to the chair.

I returned to the table with the messy pamphlets and lowered myself into the seat. *What is wrong? I feel fine. My last period was normal. Something is wrong.*

"We have news."

"Is everything okay?" I felt a small wobble in my voice.

"Yes, yes, of course. Everything is fine." A beat. "We test your urine before the exam to make sure you are not pregnant."

I cocked my head. *Wait.* A dawning, a filling of my brain, a wave of understanding spilled into my frontal cortex. *Wait.*

"Yes," she smiled. She saw the realization fill my eyes. "The test is positive. You are pregnant."

A puff of air exploded out of my nose. "What? Wait," I sputtered. "I have only been off the pill for three weeks. I've been on it for years."

"Okay, yes. I see this is a surprise." She hesitated and planted on a grin. "Have you had unprotected sex in the last three weeks?"

"Yes," I nodded. "Yes, but just a couple of times. We used condoms. It has been only three weeks. How can I be pregnant?" I rambled, the words rolling out of my mouth before my brain could stop them.

"Okay." She was patient. "This is a lot for you to take in." The kind blonde lady in the grey scrubs handed me one of the scattered pamphlets, of which I had failed to read the headline before: *Now You Are Pregnant*. "Why don't you read this, and I will be back in a few minutes."

I looked at the brochure. Not seeing it. Not seeing the words. *Now You Are Pregnant*. My brain was somehow racing and standing still at the same time. *I am pregnant? I am pregnant.*

Wait! I am pregnant? Yes. I am pregnant. I stood up, no way I could stay in the tiny room. It was shrinking. I had to move. I had to get out. *I am pregnant. Shit. I am pregnant. Wait. Are they sure?*

I charged out of the miniature room and nearly crashed into the counselor again.

"I'm sorry. I have to go."

She put a steadying hand on my arm. "Are you okay?"

"Yeah." I looked around for an escape. "Yeah, I am. I mean, yeah. Are you sure? Is the test right?"

"Let's go back and sit down and talk."

"No, no. I'm okay. I mean, as long as you are sure. I do not need to talk about it. Are you sure?" I stared her down. *Is she SURE?*

"Yes, we are sure. The accuracy of the test is quite reliable."

"Okay, okay." I tried to feel the ground under my feet. "I gotta go to class." I spun toward the exit.

"Okay, well, take the brochure and read it when you can."

I clutched the pamphlet, crushing it in my fist as I ran out. I sat in the car, stunned. *I am pregnant. I am pregnant. I am going to have to tell Matt. What is Mom going to think? Fuck, I am pregnant.*

Instead of going to class, I drove home and repeated the statement out loud a hundred times. Different inflections, different voices. I kept saying it aloud to make myself hear it.

I am pregnant.

Flash Forward: First Class

We amble down the jetway, my suitcase bumping along behind me.

"Are you excited?"

"Totally!" I answer. "And thankfully we got ahold of Ashlei!"

"Yeah." Brad shakes his head, dismissing the thought. "And let's thank the FedEx gods! I can't believe you forgot your dress."

"Me either!" I squeeze the hand of my soon-to-be husband. "The dress will be there tomorrow."

"Good thing we're not getting married until Tuesday!"

I giggle and nod to the flight attendant greeting us as I lift the roller bag over the lip of the plane door.

"Good morning."

"Good morning!"

We turn down the first aisle. Seats A and B in Row 3. First class.

"Wow! This is awesome!" I feel giddy.

"I'm excited to see what you think of first class, babe." Brad lifts his carry-on bag into the overhead compartment. I stand out of his way so he can wrestle mine up next.

"I'll take the window. I know you love the aisle." I scoot in. "Here, take my purse too and shove it up there."

Brad leans his tall, lean body over the seat and puts my bag on top of the rollers. He smiles at me and flops down into the aisle seat. "Ready to go?"

"Yeah!" I nearly shout and bounce with excitement. "This seat is incredible!"

"Just wait. It gets better." He turns his face to the flight attendant perched at our row.

"Good morning, Mr. and Mrs. Mueller," the pleasant brunette says as she looks at her clipboard. "How are you doing today?"

"Good. Good," Brad answers for us.

I grin stupidly.

"Are we celebrating something today? Is this a special trip to Hawaii?"

"Yes. We are getting married," Brad happily responds.

"Wow! Well, congratulations!"

"On the beach! In two days!"

"Wow!" she says again. "That sounds wonderful. Glad to have you on board. Can I get you a preflight drink? Champagne to celebrate?"

"Yes, that is great. Thank you."

She pivots back towards the galley behind the cockpit; I face Brad with my mouth agape. "*Whaaaat?*" My eyes are big, and I am beaming.

"Yup. I knew you'd love it."

"Champagne before we even take off? This is amazing!"

Brad takes my hand and gives it a squeeze. "You are going to love this."

"I already do."

We settle in, I in awed whimsy of all of the space, service, and gadgets in the first-class seats, Brad marveling at my joy and happy he could give me this gift. The flight from Chicago to Hawaii is long, and we are changing planes in LA. Brad got us first-class seats the whole way through. On points. First-class seats on flyer mile points is the perfect way to do it. All the luxury and spoiling of first class, but none of the cost. A perfect mix for Brad. And he could see my Christmas-morning-like joy was all the better for it.

"Nuts?" the flight attendant asks.

"Yes, please. Thank you." I nod and grin again. "This is marvelous," I say as I shove a handful of nuts in my mouth.

Brad quietly laughs beside me.

"These are warm. Oh-my-god! BRAD! Did you know these are warm?"

"Yes, babe. The nuts are warm. Enjoy."

The flight attendant puts a glass of champagne next to the nuts. "Cheers!"

A glass. A real glass. Not a plastic cup. The bubbly is in a glass.

"Do you see this?" my eyebrows raise to Brad. I tink my fingernail on the flute. "This is a REAL GLASS."

A huge smile of satisfaction plays on his face. "Yes, love, real glasses."

I feel like royalty. There is a menu! The flight attendant comes around and takes our orders. *Are you kidding me*?! Then when they bring the food, they lay a mini tablecloth on the tray, and it is complete with real china and silverware. A mini dish holds our butter, and we each have our own salt and pepper shakers. Am I dreaming? If this is heaven, I'll take it!

This was not my first flight on an airplane. I had flown tons by this time. Even as a kid, I had started flying back and forth to my dad's twice a year at six years old. I had traveled a lot for business and taken Ashlei and Olivia to Florida each year for the past five or six years. I did not have the funds to fly first class.

First class is marvelous, and my first experience is on a long flight to Hawaii to get married on the beach. It is a luxurious treat, and I relish each moment, while Brad savors my joy and wonder.

We change planes on the Big Island to a puddle jumper to get to Maui, and a rainbow stretches over the small plane. We take the rainbow as a sign, that our coming-together is meant to be so, and that life ahead will be awesome.

WOODEN SPOON

The doctors did the math and told me I'd conceived on New Year's Eve. Didn't matter when it happened. I was pregnant, due date in the fall. When I told my mom, four days after getting the news, she asked, "What do you plan to do?" I had not considered an abortion until that moment. I didn't want one. Matt was on board, and we plowed ahead. We were going to have a baby. Young and clueless, we had no idea what this meant for our lives. The semester was rough, lots of puking, and my 8:00 a.m. classes suffered, as did my grades. I started a second job at a daycare. We moved again at the end of the summer before the baby came, and I took the fall semester off.

Ashlei Nadine joined the world after fifteen hours of labor on September 19 at 3:32 p.m. At the time, we did not know what to name her. We came up with Ashley in the hospital room. Her Uncle Frank said if we were going to name her Ashley, then we should at least spell it differently.

I did not know anyone named Ashley, and neither did Matt. Apparently the name was popular in the early '90s. Frank filled out the birth certificate for us and spelled her name Ashlei. She has been plagued with everyone spelling her name wrong ever since. Plus, there are no tchotchkes with her properly spelled name on them—no key chains or bike license plates for Ashlei. We left the hospital six hours after she was born, and she has run the world ever since.

Ashlei was amazing, instantly loved and the center of everything from there on. Mom and Matt's mom, Wanda, were a huge help, and we created a patchwork of caregiving while I went back to work and back to school. My premed plans, however, were waylaid. Organic 2 and molecular biology had kicked my pregnant ass in spring semester, and now I was staring down the barrel of medical school with a baby who would be a two-year-old by the time I got there. After an hour at the academic counselor's office, I decided to switch to a nursing degree. I would graduate around the same time and essentially be guaranteed a job. After getting registered for spring semester classes, I ran into a friend.

"Hey, Hope. How's it going?"

"Super! I just registered for classes. Start in two weeks."

"What?" His jaw dropped "What are you doing?"

"Taking a bunch of nursing prerequisites."

"You're going back to school?"

"Um, yeah." I gave him a "well, duh" look. "How else am I going to finish?"

"You're finishing school?" He stared at me, incredulous.

"Yeah," I laughed and smiled. "Of course. Why wouldn't I?"

"Man, I don't know." He shook his head. "I didn't think you were going back. I'm impressed." He smothered me in a bear hug.

Ah! The proverbial light bulb popped on. I had not considered dropping out of college. The option hadn't entered my mind. I knew I was going to finish school. I knew I was going to get a degree. If anyone thought I was going to give up on my dreams, they obviously didn't know me. It might not have been evident in all parts of my life, but goals were always important. Having a baby would not stop my plans.

The prereq nursing classes proved supportive for my GPA, but the women in these classes were unkind, and I couldn't figure out how they were going to have good bedside manners. In a moment of clarity (a rare moment in my twenty-year-old brain), I thought no way I wanted these women to be my colleagues for the rest of my life. I looked beyond my immediate circumstances and projected what a life would look like working amongst these peers. Maybe it was because the program was competitive and we were young, but the women in my cohort were not friendly, and I did not want to spend my life working amongst them.

Perhaps nursing was not the vocational path for me. I went back to the academic counselor to discuss options. He indicated I only had thirty-two credits left to finish with a BS in biology. A year and a half and I would be done. That seemed doable. I switched my focus back to the more difficult coursework in biology and geared up for a hard sprint to the academic finish line. I was focused and vowed my final years of school would not suffer from my life commitments.

I worked three jobs: the daycare, a balloon store, and I started hanging wallpaper with a contractor (Who knew I would do so much wallpapering?!). The balloon store was enjoyable and, like the daycare, did not pay much. The wallpaper job was physical, paid okay, then the owner got creepy so I ditched that gig. We kept the rotation of childcare going for Ashlei between me and the two grandmothers.

Matt and I had been together only a few months when we got pregnant. By the time Ashlei was born, we knew each other about a year. Not exactly a genuine foundation to build a family. It's fair to say our "honeymoon" was over. The fun freedom of young life was long gone. Matt kept busy, but never had any money. He spent evenings out drinking and had drugs to buy. I was not a saint either. I smoked pot but steered clear of everything else. Matt and I both fawned over Ashlei, as did the grandparents, aunts, and uncles. We were in it, this makeshift relationship, without any other real connection to each other. We were scraping our lives together, lurching from one event to the next, trying to stay on task and make enough money to pay the next round of rent and bills, eking out a living, paycheck to paycheck.

Expectations evolved, especially for me. Matt became less tolerant of what I did and who I was. His way was the right way. I had to have dinner cooked each night, one protein and three sides. This is how Matt's mom prepared meals, and I was to do the same, except our financial position meant I was allowed to cook two sides without getting yelled at. The house had to be in impeccable order when he got home. There was a series of things that had to be done to prevent a derisive comment or scream fest. These included, but were not limited to, dinner had to be prepared (with requisite protein and sides); no pots, pans, or dishes on the counter or stove while we ate; no dishes in the sink overnight; the sink had to be wiped down (spotless and dried); no stray toys or papers out; everything had to be put away; my backpack had to be packed and next to the front door; the bed had to be made each morning (of course); the closet doors and all drawers had to be fully shut; the placement of the coffee table had to be at correct angles; and, very importantly, the car had to be parked in the exact precise spot. The car could not be too close to the garage, but not too far away either. These things were not too much to ask for. *Is it too much to ask to not have dishes in the sink overnight?*

The list went on (and on). I woke up early with Ashlei, got us ready and out the door. I scheduled my classes from 8:00 a.m. until noon each day and worked in the afternoons, then raced home to get dinner ready and the house tidy before Matt got home. If I wanted to play with Ashlei, I then had to do a mad dash to get everything in order and the toys cleaned up prior to him walking in the door. Honestly, I thought this was normal until one day a friend was visiting and we were playing with Ashlei. When I glanced at the clock and saw it was almost time for Matt to get home, I launched into action. I was on a mission and a race against the clock to get the house spotless.

"What are you doing, Hope? You're running around like a chicken with its head cut off!"

"Well . . ." I looked at the swaddle of clothes in my left hand and a toy in my right and shrugged. "Matt likes the house clean when he gets home."

"Do you do this every day? Are you nervous? Are you scared?"

My friend was observant and was good at getting to the heart of a matter. I issued some lame excuse, yet a seed was planted. A slow-germinating seed.

Matt was easily angered; maybe it was the drugs, maybe not. Lots of yelling and throwing things. I could fight with the best of them. Or so I thought. Money, drugs, drinking, or the messy house were all favorite topics. The violence started easy at first. No open slapping or hitting happened, but pushing and shoving were common. It was routine for me to stand in the kitchen in my jammies waiting for him to get home in the dark hours of the morning. We battled until it was time to go to school the next day. Ashlei slept in a stroller by the bed. Now I wonder how much sleep she got.

I was a tenacious person with ambition and attitude; however, dominance in the home was established. Matt was physically stronger than me. I thought I was smarter, and I thought I knew how to fight. He showed me I was wrong and I was weak.

Making life even tougher was the fact that we were poor. There were no roommates now, no extra food, no sharing of anything. I placed food strategically in the refrigerator to make it look like we had more than we did. I was levelheaded at budgeting, even though I had little to work with, and I worked nonstop. The truth was we could not afford Matt's bad habits.

The days and nights strung together. Matt was late again. I waited, fuming. Arms crossed. The couch was just inside the front door, and I sat there waiting for him to stumble into the house. The car lights passed through the front window and the gravel crunched under his tires. He parked in the open spot in front of the house. I heard the car door slam. Matt shoved open the door, and we made instant eye contact. He tossed the car keys onto the coffee table (which I had placed at the right angle, the way he wanted). His look was ebony, and the blackness hurt.

"Oh," he slurred. "So we are going to do this tonight? I guess you are not feeling 'so pink' tonight, huh?" His fingers did air quotes as he mocked me.

"Where were you?" I demanded.

"Like I am going to tell you." Matt passed through the living room and strutted into the kitchen. He thought he could ignore me.

"Where are you going?" I stood up and followed him. "You were supposed to pay the gas bill."

"So?" He fumbled for a cup.

"So? You fucker, how are we going to heat the house if we don't have gas?" I got in his face.

"I don't have any money. We can use yours." Crown Royal and spit huddled in the corners of his mouth.

"What? Are you fucking kidding me?" My voice was no longer steady. "I have paid everything and bought groceries. You were supposed to take care of the utilities. I already wrote two bad checks hoping they don't go through until I get paid on Wednesday."

"Ah, fuck you, bitch." The glassy eyes bored into me. "You haven't done shit. This fucking house looks trashed." He gestured wildly around the spotless kitchen. "You don't take care of shit." He spoke slowly. Menacingly. Something in his look changed; it scared me. I knew I'd pushed too hard and had better walk this back.

"Yeah, whatever." I pivoted to leave the kitchen back towards the living room. "I guess you can figure it out tomorrow. Borrow money from your mom or something."

"Hey!" He clamped down on my arm.

Ouch. This is gonna leave a mark.

"Don't fucking turn away from me, bitch. I don't need anything from my mom. I work for a living." Matt swayed, holding my left arm with his right and spun me to face him. I backed up and tried to twist free.

"Fucking let go of me!" I wrenched my arm, unable to loosen his grip.

"What, you dumb cunt? You fucking slob. I thought you wanted to fight." His left hand clamped down on my right shoulder. "You were waiting up for me, right?"

I pulled and rotated; it only brought him closer. His high school wrestling prowess helped. Matt was wiry and strong. Steel braids of muscle slid under his skin pulled taut with strain. He grappled me to the floor. I was face down and pinned before I could react. He shoved my face into the linoleum.

"Is this what you wanted?" His spittle bounced off my neck. "This? You wanted to fucking fight? You thought you could win, stupid bitch? You thought you would wait up for me and nag me without a fight?"

I crooked my head and tried to create some breathing room.

"Eat shit." Matt pushed my face into the floor. Straddled over my back, my arms secured beneath his knees, I was trapped. Ineffective. *Just try and breathe . . . how many red marks are going to be on my face tomorrow? Just breathe . . .*

"All right," he huffed. With another hard push to my skull, he shoved himself up. "That should be good. Dumb bitch."

I flattened out. And breathed for a second. He was right; it should have been good enough. But my rage was powered by the hours of waiting by the door, again. My blood pressure cranked with each passing quarter hour. Now the embarrassment of being restrained and my face rubbed on the floor sparked something deep. He had me down quickly, with barely a fight. *I should be stronger than this. I should be more powerful than him.* He swaggered into the passthrough bathroom, which led to the bedroom. I seized a wooden spoon and lunged through the bedroom door and whacked his ribcage.

"FUCK!" He whipped around faster than possible. "What the . . . ?"

Matt jerked the spoon from my hand and flung it backwards. He grabbed my arm, while I wailed away on his side with my free hand. Scratching. Hitting. Pounding. He clutched a handful of my hair, pulled my head back and heaved me onto the bed. I skittered back and tried to roll off the other side. He yanked my ankle and pulled me to the edge of the bed and jumped on. Flip and switch, before I could respond, I was prone. He was fast. *Fuck.*

"Is this what you fucking wanted to do, bitch? This? You fucking want to die tonight?"

Matt pushed me harder into the bed.

"Fucking hit me with a spoon? Should have gotten something sharper, stupid bitch."

He slammed my face into the bed. "You are gonna fucking die, cunt."

I was pinned. His muscled thighs held me tight against myself, his left hand on the back of my skull ramming my head into the mattress. I was still fighting. Jolting. Thrashing. Heaving. Trying to save myself. *Fuck.*

"Stop fucking fighting me. Stop trying to get up!"

With my face smashed into the mattress, suffocating in the blanket, he slid his right hand around my neck and squeezed. My thrashing slowed. *Shit.*

"Ah, that's it. That's it, isn't it, bitch?"

He looped his left arm across my throat. He gripped his own hand and pulled back. He had good leverage as I was prone on the bed, arms trapped under his legs, my body being pulled upward by my neck. No air.

"Ah, all right. Now you can't fight. Now you can't win. You fucking want to die."

He adjusted his grip, and got a firmer hold. He wrenched my neck so hard that my torso lifted off the bed. My windpipe was closed. There was no air. No breath. Nothing.

Darkness marched into my vision and thrummed in my ears. I was not fighting. *If he does not let go soon, I will pass out. If he keeps choking me, I will die.* I went limp.

He continued, insistent. Insistent on my silence. Insistent on my compliance. My death.

Blackness. No vision. No breath. Nothing.

A pounding in my ears. *How long had it been since I had a breath? How long is he going to choke me? Hopefully I pass out soon. Peace.*

I am nothing. Compliant.

Maybe he thought I died. Maybe he got bored without me fighting. He let go and slid off of me.

Light bloomed back into my vision, and I coughed. Choking and sucking in air. Breathing. Hacking. Eyes watering.

He stumbled out of the bedroom into the living room.

"Dumb bitch. Got what you deserve." Matt rummaged for the keys from the perfectly placed coffee table, and I heard the front door open and close.

I took a deep breath and rolled onto my side. Tears

slipped down my cheeks. The drumming faded, the quiet brought a newfound understanding.

The car engine roared, and the tires squelched.

This is how it is.

He can kill me.

He will kill me.

FLASH FORWARD: VP

I pull into the parking lot thirty minutes early, common for me. I hate to be late. I flip down the visor and slide Burt's Bees red dahlia lip balm on my lips. Okay. I look okay.

Not wanting to be too early, I wait in the car for fifteen minutes. Fifteen minutes shows timeliness and preparation. I hold my jacket close around me as I walk into the big building. Another cold, grey March day in Northern Illinois.

The building looks like a typical corporate office in these suburbs. Not a towering high-rise that you might see in the city, this is four stories, a reflective-glass-clad slate grey edifice. I rotate through the revolving door. There is no reception in the main foyer, no security. I spy a bathroom sign.

I wash my hands and do a final check. Black slacks, grey blouse, and black jacket, a women's business uniform. New shoes finish the outfit. Long ago I read to wear shoes in good condition to an interview. I figured new shoes were my best bet. Perhaps bring me some luck.

The directory in the lobby points me to Suite 150. I swing open one of the two large frosted glass doors. There is an empty reception desk.

"Hello?" A smiling blonde rounds the corner. "Can I help you?"

"Yes! I'm here to meet with Ronald for an interview."

"Ah, right." She nods and moves to her desk. "I will get him for you. You can take a seat."

I sit on the edge of a chair and glance at the pharma publications on the glass table. I do a self-inventory. *Am I nervous?* Not really, more excited. I click through my reminders: Say exactly what needs to be said, nothing more, nothing less; do not be too enthusiastic or "passionate," as this is a vice president role and I have to show *executive presence*; and be a good listener. The best advice for interviews, especially when interviewing with people in the C-Suite, is to listen.

The blonde comes back out, introduces herself, and we shake hands. She leads me down the hall and offers me water or coffee.

"A water would be great. Thank you."

We stop into a kitchenette, and she hands me a bottle of water. She then leaves me in a large conference room. "Okay, here you are. Ronald will join you in a minute."

"Thank you."

The table is dark wood, shiny in finish. Twelve huge black leather chairs encircle it. A crazy-looking leather statue sits atop a credenza. I put my foldered resumes on the end of the table and drop my purse into a chair. Framed prints of the Chicago sports venues are hung prominently. I walk around the room and look at Wrigley Field, The Cell, and The United Center.

I hear a door open behind me, and I turn to greet the person entering.

"Hi, I'm Hope."

"Yes." He smiles. "I'm Ronald."

We shake hands. Firm grip, steady look in the eye, easy natural smile.

"Take a seat." He gestures to the chair where my folder sits. He lowers himself into the chair across from me.

Ronald interviews me for about an hour. He tells me about the company and shares the interview panel for the day. I meet most everyone who works at the company; it is a small home office. As the day stretches on, they add people to the panel, and I am interviewed through lunch. Everyone seems friendly and wicked smart. I'm a little nervous talking with the CEO, but he puts me at ease with a down-to-earth, comfortable style. I think it is going well.

I realize I am excited and probably too "passionate" by the afternoon. It's hard for me to hold it in for a whole day. I am energetic. I am excitable. I love talking about work and getting things done.

By 3:30 in the afternoon, I've talked with eight or nine people when Ronald comes back to close the discussion.

"Well, how did the day go?" He grins at me.

"Good!" I smile and laugh a little. "I don't know! You tell me."

"Oh, I think you are right. I think it went great." Ronald takes a seat, and I sit down too. "It's important for you to talk to the team. This is a small office, and if the wrong type of person comes in, it disrupts the whole team."

"Yeah, I can imagine." I wait to see where he is going.

"The good news is the whole team liked you." A wide smile spreads across his face. Ronald extends his hands on the table. "Theodore (the CEO) liked you. We think you are a great fit for us."

I nod. I don't want to blow it and say something stupid.

"We want to offer you the job." He turns his hands upward. "Do you think you want to join the team?"

"What? That is awesome!" I burst out, so un-vice-president-like. "Yes! Let's do it!" I try to be level and calm.

We talk title and pay. We talk start dates. Ronald states they will have the formal written offer to me by the end of the week.

This had never happened to me before, being offered a job on the spot. There are usually a few days of waiting and wondering, never really certain if the interview went well or not, until you hear back. This was the first time I was offered the job at the interview. Ronald explained the company's size made them nimble, and they could make an offer quickly when they liked a candidate. They wanted me to start as soon as possible.

Start date was important to me too. I had to give a long-ish notice. In the organization I was leaving, I had over 120 people with 10 direct reports and sat on the senior leadership team of the site. I needed to put together a transition plan, interim leaders, and make sure my team was taken care of as much as possible in my departure.

In April 2015, I was back in Suite 150 in the grey glass-clad building, wearing those same new shoes, now in my first vice president role.

MAGIC EIGHT BALL

A near death experience changes you. Or at least shapes you. When Matt choked me that night, my mind was quiet, accepting. There was no panic, simply a full sense of calm. A matter-of-factness. *I may die. If he does not stop, I may be dead.* My body had no escape, so my mind accepted the truth.

I did not cross over into the other side, there was no white light, or other experience. There was a peace. A strange peace with this life possibly ending. I don't know what it meant, but that is was what I felt. No fear, no panic, no life flashing before my eyes, only a realization and acceptance of my pending death.

I stayed.

I did not tell anyone, not my mom, not my friends. No one.

I did not love or hate Matt any more or any less after the event. I did *know*, though. I knew what he was capable of and who he was. And it did change our relationship. His dominance was cemented. I knew he was stronger and faster than me. I pushed less hard, stood my ground less and less, and diminished myself to comply. I had already been moving in that direction, and being choked expedited my shrinking. I did what I could to keep the peace. I stayed. The psychology of it is twisted.

At school and at work, however, I was not shrinking. I was growing. In the throes of a hard push to the finish line for my degree, I took between thirteen to sixteen credit hours a semester and held two jobs. My grades were serviceable, not great, but I was doing it. I was passing. Between my junior and senior years, I took summer classes. The whole experience was compressed, and the credit hours racked up.

My first summer session lasted six weeks, and the second session eight. I completed physics II, statistics, a writing class, and a criminal justice class because I was curious about it, not because it was required. Ashlei went with me to some of these classes. We set up in the back of the room with a coloring book and crayons. She was not disruptive, and only once did I have to take her out because she was getting rambunctious. The professors did not mind, and it helped get me closer to the degree.

Needing a flexible schedule and more cash than I was making at the balloon store, I joined the debauchery at

Nick's, the historic tavern on the IU campus where my mom had once worked. I was twenty, and my job was carding people at the door. Long lines wrapped around the bar on game days. The young kids with fake IDs were always easy to spot. Lots of cajoling and attempted bribery happens at the door of a bar. I was impervious and unruffled. I stood my ground and could look people in the eye and either let them in or not. It also was not lost on me that I could be commanding everywhere except at home. Matt settled down, sort of. I toed the line. He didn't stop his bad behaviors, but we had fallen into some kind of warped normalcy.

After I turned twenty-one, I started waitressing. Servers brought home a lot of money, and I certainly could use it. At first, I got the crappy shifts and the slow Monday nights upstairs, but even that shift grew profitable because I had a crew of regulars who tipped me well.

As junior year sailed into senior year, I felt crunched. Full-time school, full-time work, and taking care of Ashlei and the home was a lot. I did not have time to spend with friends; my life was Ashlei, school, work, and trying to do what Matt wanted. Matt and I moved often too, trying to stay in a budget. We had to financially stretch to make ends meet, driving crappy cars, never having money for groceries. Matt's prism of jobs kept turning, and his drug use intensified. He didn't spend much time with Ashlei, but when he did, he played with her. His role was the fun dad, and he loved her.

The pot smoking did not bother me much. I grew up with it, the way many families drink alcohol. It was the other stuff he was doing, the alcohol and the racers, that put extra strain on the family. Meth, cat, or crack, I am not sure what it is called, was a cheaper form of cocaine, and his friend made it in his trailer in a rural neighboring county. Matt wasn't just an occasional user. He was a frequent flyer.

I still smoked pot occasionally. I was too busy with my responsibilities to party too much. The 400-level classes in a rigorous science degree were not easy, and I didn't have much time to study. To be successful (pass), I had to do one thing: go to class. So I went to class, paid full attention, and took robust notes. I studied two or three days leading up to an exam, and that is all it took for a passing grade. I no longer went to study groups or other activities that might have helped me academically. I was hanging on and aiming for graduation.

Matt never gave me a hard time for going to school. He supported the goal. We both knew it was a ticket out. He had never finished college. I would finish. Damn, I would if my life depended on it. My life, Ashlei's life, our family's financial life depended on me graduating. The pressure was mounting, and I was worn out. Drained by the late nights at the bar, getting off at two or three, then getting up for an eight o'clock class, I was running on fumes.

One night, I was humping it upstairs in the busy college kids' section at Nick's, and Matt was at the front bar where the regulars hung out. I was beat. He came upstairs to see me.

"I want to go home. I want to tell them I quit. I am dying," I said, my voice a whimper.

"Ah, you've got this, Hope. You have been doing this for years. You're fine," Matt replied.

"Matt," I pleaded. "I can't. I'm tired. How am I going to make it through another semester?" I frowned and took a deep breath. "I don't know if I can finish school and work here too."

A moment of realization passed over his face, a glimmer of understanding. He saw I was struggling. I never complained, so how would he know I was so whacked? Instead of getting angry, Matt softened.

"Look, Hope, you can do this." He glanced around. "Hon, I know you are worn out. But you're too close to not get this done. Where else are you going to work where you will get paid this much?"

It was true. I was now working the best three nights a week, and I picked up extra shifts on game days, which helped our finances. There was nowhere else I could work and make this kind of money. Maybe another bar. Which would be no better than the situation now.

"Jeez, I don't know." I scanned the room checking my tables. Did everyone have drinks? Who needed ketchup? Were they ready for their check? I felt tears coming on. *Shit. Suck it up.*

Matt took both of my hands in his. "I just got an eight ball," he said in a low whisper. "You want to try it? It will help you finish your shift and give you a boost of energy."

I scrunched up my face. I was dead tired and on the verge of breaking down in the middle of my shift, but I did not need this new wrinkle in my life.

"No. No drugs. I will get some coffee." I pulled my hands from his grip and rubbed a hand across my forehead, pulling the hair away from my face. "I gotta shake it off."

"Are you sure? He glanced around again conspiratorially. "We can chop it up in the storage room. I do it all the time."

"Nah, I'm fine." I spun away to check on the table of frat boys; it looked like their pitcher of Bud Light was getting low. Being a waitress is physical; you are on your feet moving the whole night. There was no shortage of mental challenges too. There are drunk patrons you have to coddle to get the best tip, but you can't overserve them, and not be too chummy or flirty. Dog-tired and bone-weary, I did not do lines that night, and it was not the first time Matt had offered drugs to me. It was, however, the first time I considered it.

I resisted the temptation of the jolt of energy I thought the coke would give me. But not long after, I was wiped out, ready to drop, and I succumbed. Matt showed me how to chop up the rock with a razor blade, roll up a dollar bill, and snort it.

It was a Thursday morning after a long night shift. Matt was doing lines before going to work, and I had an early morning class. The coke was better than coffee. It was like a thousand coffees, and it perked me right up. I flew through my class schedule, nearly running from one class to the next. Hyper aware, I felt like the smartest, most crisp, alert student in class (probably was). I came home in the afternoon and even spent some time studying. I got so much done that day.

Matt came home before I had to go to my evening shift, and I got another bump. *Yes!* This is great. I am awake! I am alert! I was the most attentive, on-top-of-it server there ever had been. I did my "twelve o'clock shot" with the bartender at midnight and was still flying high. This was great. It was exactly what I needed. When I got home, I fell asleep hard and quick, which was not normal for me. It usually took me forever to quiet my mind and go to sleep. Whoa! This was perfect. It was a ray of hope. I could finish school and this grueling schedule if I had a little help from the magic eight ball.

The problem with drugs, especially speedy drugs, is that it takes more and more to get the same effect. The first day was perfection. I was awake all day, hyper alert, and the best student and waitress I had ever been. One bump in the morning, like coffee, and one before my shift was all I needed. Honestly, and obviously, I had not thought it through.

I enjoyed the first day and figured it was a way for me to get enough pep to get through my life. I did not plan to use all of the time, just when I needed a boost. I did not plan to become addicted and sacrifice my money, time, and child. That isn't how addicts start out using. No one plans to become a drug addict.

Exhausted the next day, I had to go to class Friday morning and work another shift at Nick's that night. I did not want to do more drugs. I thought, *Well, just for today.* Just to get through class then work.

It was January when I did coke that fateful Thursday morning, and by March I was using every day. Every single day.

I had an emptied pressed powder compact and snuggled a small twisted up baggie with a rock in it, plus a tiny straw, cut to size, wedged neatly in there. The compact bounced around in my backpack with me everywhere. I carried this to class and did lines in the biology building bathrooms. The bathrooms on the third and fourth floors were usually empty, and no one noticed me. I switched up the bathrooms and places I snuck into in order to avoid suspicion—and because speed makes you paranoid.

At Nick's I did lines in the bathroom, backroom, or storage room. I didn't have to be too careful there because most of the workers did drugs. The trick at work was doing it so I did not have to share.

No longer was one bump in the morning and afternoon going to get me through the day; I needed more. Up to this point, I don't know how Matt kept this addiction below critical mass. He had used cocaine for years without getting into massive daily use. The meth changed the variables. It was cheaper, he had more access, and it may have had higher addiction properties. He had been using every day for a while, and I joined him.

We slid downhill. Both of us used every day. We spent all of our extra money on it. Life unraveled faster and faster, along with my racing heartbeat.

ANOTHER THURSDAY

It was another Thursday. I stood at the Planned Parenthood counter, the same one I had been at before, and each year since I was sixteen. The office had changed little, the bowl of condoms and the same teal green chairs were still there. Every year I went for an annual exam to get a prescription for birth control. The three weeks I went without birth control when I was nineteen resulted in a pregnancy. Resulted in Ashlei. The first time, I was clueless. This time was different. Anxiety cranked my nerves, and I felt like a jumpy cat. I was shaking. And I knew I was pregnant.

There is an unidentifiable shift in my body when I become pregnant. My boobs are heavy. I smell different. There is a change, an invisible transformation of cells, something unspecific and hard to describe, with a definite knowing. At home I had taken the pregnancy test even though the kit was expensive. The kit had two test sticks in the box, so I did the second one to confirm the first one. I was maniacal about taking birth control, never missing a pill, and taking them the same time every day. Here I was. The second stick showed what the first one said.

Shit.

Deep into addiction, I was doing lines of meth two-three-four-five times a day. And had been for several weeks by this time. This is what "clean" people do not understand or know about addicts. Addicts do their drugs and go on living their life. We tend to think of addicts holding a brown bag on the side of the road, homeless and disheveled. Maybe that's some, but I assure you, addicts are around you all the time. The addicts who are homeless or strung out are on the tail end of a long road and lengthy time of addiction. An addict who fits the stereotypical image takes years to get that way. Leading up to it are the people you know and interact with every day.

People who have never been addicted don't know those around them are addicts, but we recognize it in others. We see it in their eyes, in their off-hand comments, and the way they move. Addicts know the signs of addiction, intuitively, because we know their struggle.

I was not *yet* a back-alley junkie living in a gutter or in a car. I was going to school and working. Functioning. My grades were good, even though I was doing heavy drugs. I passed all of my classes that semester—300- and 400-level biology course work, including biochemistry and microbiology laboratory classes. I hadn't missed class. I hadn't missed shifts at work. I had missed my period.

Shit.

I had been doing drugs daily for weeks now. I took the birth control pills daily too. Every fucking day, at the same time. And the pregnancy test said it's positive. *Fuck no. How is this possible?*

The zygote, which might be a blastocyst by this time, had been exposed to methamphetamine consistently since inception. Every damn day. The fertilized egg embedded in the uterine wall, this blastocyst, had been absolutely and heavily exposed to drugs and alcohol. *How had this impacted the development? How had I gotten pregnant? I had not missed a day of birth control! Maybe the meth impacted the effectiveness of the hormones in the birth control? How did this happen?!*

It can obviously be extrapolated the blastocyst was harmed by my addiction. By the methamphetamine. The blood, my blood, carried the drugs and fed them to the placenta and uterine wall. Was the blastocyst an embryo yet? Would I have a spontaneous miscarriage because of the drug use?

I took the pregnancy test on Friday night at home. *Shit.* First thing Saturday morning, I called the clinic. The decision was immediate with the reveal of the ++ on the stick.

I could not carry this blastocyst to term. I was an addict. Even if I stopped drugs immediately, the damage had been done. You cannot reverse or undo what had been done. You cannot undo drug use.

The person on the other end of the phone said it was mandatory to take a pregnancy test in the clinic. I planned to go in on Monday morning, then schedule the abortion for Thursday. On Monday, I left the sample. The clinic confirmed the pregnancy, yet I somehow hoped to start my period throughout the week. Monday, Tuesday, and Wednesday passed with no blood in my underwear.

Matt agreed on the abortion. He barely even registered the discussion. It was my problem to handle, same as most of our family problems. When we got pregnant the first time, we both knew exactly what to do with no debate. We knew we were going to have Ashlei. We did not even discuss an abortion the first time. This time, again, we knew what to do with no debate.

I knew it was the right choice. Sometime during class that week I shared my story with a study partner in my biochemistry class. I left out the drug use part, though maybe she could tell. She said nothing, just listened. I don't remember the full conversation. I did tell her the decision I had made.

I had been yelled at by the crazies with their placards of aborted fetuses before going into the Planned Parenthood office on prior visits. It is outrageous that a human would do this to another human. Shout at them, scream in their face, as they seek medical care. Those protestors have no idea why a woman might be going into a clinic; it could be for anything. They presume they know. They don't know her life. They don't know anything about her. They yell at her and call her names. It is evil, and it should be illegal. I had been harassed in the past, going in for an annual exam and birth control, but this Thursday no one was there screaming at me, and I was there to get an abortion.

I took a seat in a dirty teal green chair. The same green teal chairs. A nurse in green scrubs called my name. I wobbled to my feet and shuffled behind her.

"Hello, Hope. How are you feeling today?"

"A bit nervous. I'm okay though."

"Good. Good." She walked confidently to a small exam room. "Before we can do the procedure, we will do an intravaginal ultrasound. Are you familiar with that?"

"Yes. I have had one of those before."

The nurse handed me a folded paper gown and drape. "Please completely undress and put this on. The opening is in the front. The drape can go across your lap."

"Okay," I took the gown and waited for her to leave. My hands shook as I undressed. I folded my clothes precisely and tucked my panties under the folded jeans and placed my clothing pile on a small chair. I climbed up onto the table and sat on the edge and waited. The room was dim. Ultrasound rooms are dim so the technician can see the images. I had done this before, then excited and hopeful for the embryo in my belly. This day felt different. Sketchy, is how I felt, sketchy. Staticky as an Etch A Sketch screen. Grey fuzz buzzed in my mind. My eyes flitted around the room waiting for the nurse or a technician to enter.

A soft knock on the door. "Are you ready?" the voice beyond the door asked. "May I come in?"

"Yeah."

The technician unfolded the stirrups from their hiding place in the table. I laid back, then scooted my butt to the furthest most edge. She guided my feet into the cool touch of the stirrups, my heel resting on the edge and the metal bar traversing the middle of my foot.

I took a steeling breath. A calming breath. I closed my eyes. I did not want to see.

"Okay, you will feel pressure. I am inserting the wand."

When I was pregnant with Ashlei, I eagerly stared at the monitor trying to make sense out of the shapes and curves on the grey-white-black screen. This time I did not want to see. With Ashlei, I could hear the woosh, woosh, woosh of her heartbeat. There was no sound in this room.

When the wand stopped moving and pushed hard, I could not help myself. I knew the monitor was glowing and facing me. I looked. I saw the blinking of the miniature cardiac muscle. It flashed white/black/white/black. There was no shape, no identity, only a flashing in a blob of white.

She held the wand there and took measurements. Click. Click. Click. Adjusting the wand again, click, click, click. I stared at the blinking mass. I threw my head back onto the table, closed my eyes, and took another breath. The tears welled. Then rolled.

"All right. It looks like we got what we need." She removed the wand and wiped it off. "You can sit up now and get dressed. I'll take these to the doctor, who will review these images. Then we will call you back in."

"Okay," I heard myself utter. The static itched my skull. "Okay." She left the room, and I tremored putting my clothes back on. The tears were hard now, silent. Sniffing back the snotty drain, I rubbed the back of my hand across my nose. Sniffed it in. I took another deep breath, pulled my shoulders back, and opened the door.

A nurse was there. She guided me to a back waiting room, smaller, with the same aged teal green chairs with wooden arms. "You can wait here."

I slumped into the seat. The tears had not abated and were flowing freely now. I sniffed loudly and tried to be quiet while I cried.

Someone took my hand. Startled, I looked up to see the girl from class. The one I told my story. I did not even know her name. My crying turned into heavy sobs, racking my body. She sat down next to me and held my hand and wrapped her arm around my shoulders. I cried. She cried too. I don't know how long we were there. I don't know if anyone else was in the small waiting room.

"Hope? Hope?" A new nurse called my name. Yellow folder in hand, same green scrubs.

"Yes." I stood up. My friend stood with me, and clutched my hand. "Yes." I shook off the static. I shook off the tears.

"We are ready. Are you ready?"

"Yes." I faced the girl from class, and we hugged. For seconds, enough seconds for some strength. She gave my shoulders a quick squeeze. I looked at her and tried to convey my gratitude. She left. I never saw her again. I still do not know her name.

In through the nose, out through the mouth, I closed my eyes with this deep breath, then opened my eyes again to follow the nurse into another exam room. This room was well-lit. Same table, I know the stirrups were hidden in the edge of this one too. There was a large machine on the right side of the table. A non-descript machine. A large box, blinking red lights on the top, with a wand secured to the side. The unit looked the same as the ultrasound machine without a monitor. The nurse and I go through the same procedure with the drape and the open-front gown.

Then a tap on the door.

"Yes."

"Hello." A middle-aged man entered with a green-scrubbed nurse close behind. The doctor introduced himself with a firm handshake and even stare. "Are you ready to do this today?"

"Yes."

He slid his eyes sideways to the nurse. "Nancy here says you were upset in the waiting room."

"Yes. But I am okay now." I am. I am okay. Resolute.

"All right, then." He nodded and settled onto a stainless-steel stool. "What we are going to do is insert the speculum, the same as a routine exam. Then we are going to use this dilator to open up your uterus." He held up a tube-looking thing. "Then we are going to insert this device into your uterus and scrape out the placenta and scrape the uterine wall." Still nodding and looking me in the eye, he asked, "Okay?"

"Okay."

"Any questions?"

"No."

"Okay, let's get started then." He whipped around on the stool and put on gloves. "Please lay back."

I lay back and scooted to the edge of the table, again. The nurse unfolded the stirrups and guided my feet to them, again. The chilly speculum was inserted. The doctor cranked down the bolt and tightened the hold on the speculum. The dilator felt like a small pinch. He switched on the machine, which sounded like a vacuum.

"Okay, we are going to remove the placenta now. Okay? Are you okay?"

"Yes."

The wand was inserted. It was like a straw. A vacuum with a wide straw on the end. It did not hurt, there was a pressure, a little more than a mild cramp. Minutes. It happened fast.

"All right. I think we are clear." He removed the straw wand, and the nurse turned off the whirring of the machine. He expertly untightened the speculum and gently removed it.

"How do you feel? Are you okay?"

"Yes."

"All right. Let's go ahead and skootch up and sit up."

I do so. *Shhhwhwhwhwhwh.* The static ticks in my mind.

"Nancy is going to give you the after-procedure instructions. Make sure to follow what she shares with you. Okay?"

"Okay."

Another handshake, and he was gone. The nurse instructed. I pretended to listen. Blankness blotted out my conscious mind. *I need to get out of here. I need to go.* I nodded at her and said yes in all the right places.

"All right, let's get dressed, and we will get you out of here." She handed me several papers and left the room.

I slammed on my clothes, racing to get out of there. *I need to go.* I laced up my tennis shoes and gripped the papers in my hand and burst out of the exam room door. Stopping at the counter with the bowl of condoms, the woman said they did not need anything from me, and I speed-walked out the door.

The sun was bright and the air cool, fresh. It soothed my staticky brain. I walked to my car. I did not cry.

I did not look back.

Flash Forward:
Legacy Statement

Seven-fifteen in the morning, and the cold air whips about my legs. I hustle into the glass conclave of the building and attempt to straighten my wind-whipped hair. The Executive Women in Healthcare programs are typically breakfast events. The morning slot works better with our busy calendars because we can meet before the day gets started. If these gatherings were booked in the afternoon, something would inevitably pop up—seemingly more important than investing in self-development.

Entering the conference room, I see the hot breakfast and coffee stations are in operation, and women are mingling. I unload my bag and briefcase onto the classroom table and clip on the name tag. More coffee is in order.

"Good morning!" I hug Ruth. "Thank you for organizing this one. It looks like we are going to have a great turnout."

"Yes, I agree." She scans the full room. People are networking, eating, and the room has a soft warm buzz.

"I love these breakfast sessions. Great way to start the day. And perfect for my schedule."

Coffee and fruit in hand, I chat with a few colleagues. I introduce myself to a few new people, we discuss our roles, and exchange cards. I refill my coffee cup, add a splash of cream, and settle into my seat. I check both my cell phones to confirm I have not missed anything urgent. I flip through the notebook resting on the table. The small binder has the speaker's branding, with bullet points of the content she will be reviewing and a few pages to take notes. I dig through my bag for a pencil and turn to the first page.

"Good morning, everyone," Ruth says, welcoming the crowd. "We're glad you could join us today on this chilly morning. We are going to start on time, so we can finish on time." Small knowing smiles ripple through the room. "The executive committee has put this program together based on your interest areas survey. I know you will enjoy the information and exercises. I have seen Peggy speak before, and you are in for a treat. We don't always take time to invest in ourselves or think about where we are, who we are, and where we want to be. Let's commit this morning to this discussion, so phones and laptops away."

After listing the speaker's accomplishments, Ruth introduces her. Peggy launches into her material. She is energetic, but not overly so. She hits the right tone. The crux of the content is it's important for us as female executives to be planful in establishing our personal and professional goals. This is not a foreign concept, seeing how the women in the room have already achieved a measure of corporate success—only directors and above are included in this membership. However, today's session forces us to compose a legacy statement.

A legacy statement represents your vision and aspiration for what you wish to accomplish and how you want to be remembered in life and in your organization. The speaker leads us through a series of simple concepts. We work independently on three primary goals or cornerstones of who we are and what we want to be, then discuss it with a partner at our table. Next, we are given individual time to compose a legacy statement of our own, which we will share and discuss with a different partner.

I hunker down with pencil and paper, pondering the ideas she has shared. *What is my legacy statement? Who do I want to be?* As I reflect on this, I realize I already have a legacy statement.

About ten years prior, I had written a simple sentence for myself that had served as my guiding principle for the last decade. I imagine it's common for women to wrestle with their identity after a life-changing event. For me, sometime after the divorce, I was compelled to write it down. I wanted to be clear on who I was and what I wanted to become. Only now, as I sit in this conference room, with professional executive women, do I realize I had created a "legacy statement."

My sentence had been a vision for my life. I had written this sentence everywhere. Each new notebook and journal had it in the first pages. Often, I wrote the sentence on index cards then posted them in my office and the console of the car. These words were written to myself as a reminder of who I wanted to be.

My statement was: "I am a successful, powerful, beautiful career woman and loving mother."

The time is ticking in this morning meeting, and I have not written anything down. *Okay, I already have a legacy statement, yay me.* I decide I should take this time to refresh the one I've had for all these years. Is this still the identity I want? Is this still me?

I make an addition: "I am a successful, powerful, beautiful career woman and loving *wife* and mother." I am now in a second marriage, so I want to include the word wife.

Saying I want to be beautiful may sound conceited, but I do want to think of myself as beautiful. I want to honor the beauty I do have; I want to have a healthy body and mind. I want to have a beautiful soul that emits light and joy for anyone I interact with—beautiful as a state of mind, not limited to a physical beauty.

Powerful indicates the strength and confidence I want to own, especially after the smallness I felt as a person during the years with Matt. I want to have my own power and be my own person.

The other parameters seem self-explanatory.

I have achieved this.

I look at what I can now call my legacy statement, which I wrote sometime in 2004 or 2005, and say, *Yes, this is me.* I am successful. I am powerful, at least I am my own person, and I am confident. I am beautiful. Sure, I could stand to lose a few pounds, but I'm beautiful. I am kind and spend a lot of time trying to be a positive force in the world. I am definitely a career woman and a loving wife and mother. So, okay, yes, this is me.

Then I add one more item: "I am a successful, powerful, beautiful career woman, *New York Times* bestselling author, and loving wife and mother."

This statement covers all of my bases, yet feels incomplete and is starting to look like a run-on sentence. The speaker asks us to share our legacy statements with a new partner. The woman in front of me turns around, and we discuss her statement first. She shares hers and tells me why it is important to her. I start to share mine, but we run out of time. The program ends, and we all say our goodbyes.

Off to work, this concept of legacy statement plays in the back of my mind all day. I had recently spoken at my dad's funeral and shared what I thought was his legacy. He was a teacher. No matter who interacted with him, they walked away feeling smarter, better, and more informed.

What about me? After ten years of the guiding statement

I had, I believe it's time for me to refresh it and draft a new one. In the process of creating a new legacy statement, I ended up creating three, maybe four. One does not seem enough.

My foundational legacy statements:

"Everyone who knows, interacts, or works with me will leave encouraged, inspired, developed, and loved."

"I am a loving wife, mother, and grandmother."

"I am a force for good."

Then I add some specific goals:

"I am a *NYT* bestselling author, chief operating officer (or general manager), and active not-for-profit leader in my community."

These statements are a mix of current and aspirational desires.

Whatever the language, whatever the intent, I am amazed. Amazed that I had already established a legacy statement and that I could claim some level of being what I set out to be.

I'm also happily surprised that it is clear to me it's time to push harder, to be broader, to spread my wings even more. I can do more, be more, and accomplish more with the success I have achieved—it gives me further reach.

MAY DAY

Ashlei spent a ton of time with Matt's mom or at my mom's house. When she was home, it was tenuous. When I slept, I slept hard, my body trying to gain some energy back from the racetrack I was running with the drugs and my responsibilities. Ashlei was often left unattended in the morning while I slept. She was two and a half. One morning she wrote all over her room with lipstick. Other mornings she was plopped in front of the TV or in her corner "reading" a pile of books. It was unfair to Ashlei, and unsafe. Matt and I were lost to our addiction and not good parents.

When Matt and I weren't getting high and fucking the night away, we were fighting. Our fights led out into the street, along with physical battles inside. We raged around the condo, throwing things, me being wrestled to the ground. And the screaming. The constant yelling. Pushing, shoving. A destroyed home around us. The emotional roller coaster of an addict is real. The serotonin levels are skewed in the brain. Nothing is working right; it is all short-circuiting. Matt moved in and out of our place during this period, which was great, because then I could get free meth from his dealer.

I was out of control. I lost a ton of weight, which I loved. I was not healthy.

One night, Mom sat me down and told me I was fucking up and had to get right. Ha! She was her own addict, and I had not the ears to hear her. She was the pot calling the kettle black. Matt's mom got in our business too, and threatened to take Ashlei from me. Wanda said I was an unfit mom, that Ashlei was not safe with me. I rebelled against this. Fuck that bitch. She was evil and wanted to take my daughter. Ashlei was fine. She was fine. I was fine. I was going to school and getting good grades. I worked full time. I had her at daycare, was paying for it myself. I was doing it all. Fuck Wanda.

As things spiraled, the bills started slipping. I got a credit card offer in the mail, with a $350 credit limit. You know how much an eight ball was? Yup, $350. I activated the card and promptly took the $350 out in cash and bought an eight ball. Shit, it would last me two to three days. If I could stretch it that long. Maybe, if I did not have to share it with Matt or any coworkers. It was unlikely I would make it through day two with any of it left. Fuck. This was bad. I mean, this was unsustainable. The math does not work. The use outpaces the funds fast. It is a negative regression model.

My curiosity surfaced and drove me to the library. I started researching meth, coke, and amphetamines and their effects on the brain and body. I was trying to reach myself. Trying to inform myself what I was doing to my mind. I forced myself to look at pictures of people who were destroyed by meth. Gone from beautiful young people to gaunt, black-toothed, pock-marked Halloween masks of people. I was deep into this addiction versus self-instruction when Jamaica, my old friend and roommate, came to Bloomington for a visit.

Jamaica looked at me, saw the destruction of my life, and the emaciated body. I told her how Wanda was threatening to take Ashlei from me.

"Hope," Jamaica said quietly. "She's right, you know."

"What?!" I was shocked. Jamaica was my friend.

"She's right. Do you think you are taking care of Ashlei? Do you think you are in your right mind?"

"I don't know. I mean, yes. I can take care of Ashlei just fine."

"How much are you doing? Do you do it every day?"

"No. Yes. I mean, no." I hesitated. "Yes, but it's fine. I'm fine."

"Are you? You look wasted. You look tired. I have been

here two days and you have not stopped with that." She gestured to the compact.

I was mostly coherent. It was morning, and I had taken my first bump of the day. I was not racing yet, more like a cup or two of coffee. I leaned back in the chair and tried to breathe. Tried to catch a clear thought.

"I don't know. Maybe you're right. Maybe I am doing too much." I rested my forearm across my eyes, talking into my armpit. "I have been reading about what it does to your brain. I know I need to stop."

"You do. You do need to stop. You are going to lose Ashlei." Jamaica paused for effect. "And you should." She continued. "You should lose her. You are not taking care of her, and she is not safe. You are not taking care of yourself."

I shifted in the chair, bringing my knees to chest and hugging my legs. "I thought I was doing fine. School. Work. Ashlei. The house. Matt. I thought I was doing fine."

"Look, Hope, I love you. I have always loved you." She rested her hand atop my knees that I was hiding behind. "I hate seeing you like this. This is not who you are." She stroked my hair. "I am worried you will lose Ashlei. You might die. Who would take care of Ashlei then?"

The conversation was honest, true. Jamaica did love me. I could hear it. She got through to me. I had been pretending to listen to the same advice from others who loved me. It is unfortunate that kids (young adults) don't listen to their parents, don't listen to the people who love them and want to see them safe and healthy. A peer telling you the same thing is meaningful. I had not been really taking it in, not really hearing anything when my mom told me the same things. I read about the truth. I saw pictures of the truth. And now I was ready to hear. To do something.

Jamaica saved my life. Saved me from myself. Jamaica took a risk, as a friend, and told me the truth. Her honesty was powerful and reached me. She told me she wanted me to get well, to stop doing drugs. It did not matter that everyone else, except Matt, wanted the same for me. It mattered that *she* said it. Jamaica had been a pot smoker and drug user when we were teens. It meant something coming from her. She knew me, knows me. She loved me, loves me. Jamaica saved me by being willing to tell me to get right.

I took her words to heart, and I did not use for a few days. I slipped when school and work piled up. I started using less, though, and my mind began to function again. As the fog of the addiction began to clear, I saw how I was losing my daughter and creating an unsafe home for her. Wanda had not yet engaged legal counsel. Mom supported Wanda's position that Ashlei shouldn't be with me. Mom did not push as hard because she didn't want me losing custody, but she did want me to get well and tried to tell me to get sober.

I had a choice. My daughter or drugs. Good or evil. I

distilled it down to the simplest of terms. Light or darkness. Ashlei or meth. Was I willing to knowingly, consciously choose drugs over my daughter? It was simple. The choice was black and white. It was straightforward. Drugs or my child? I made the choice. I chose Ashlei. I chose my daughter.

Although I was weaning myself off, I couldn't do it alone. With the help of Wanda's church, I started seeing a Christian drug counselor. I went to talk with him once a week. The first visit went well. I confided my quick demise, the first taste in January and by March using every day. The counselor and I agreed to the rules of our relationship. We outlined what the commitment to myself and my daughter was to be. Full stop. No drugs. No pot. Nothing. I would stop doing drugs altogether. I had to stop to save myself. To be a good mom. To take care of me and Ashlei.

On the second visit, I lied. His first question was had I used since we had last met. I reported I did, but I lied to him about how much. I told him I used three days. The truth was I had used five out of the seven days since my last appointment. *Shit*, I thought to myself, *this won't work if I lie to the person who is supposed to help me get sober.* And when I allowed myself to be honest, five out of seven days was a lot. Two days without use. And this was the meth, not pot. I used five times. Shit. I chose again. I chose good. I chose light. I chose Ashlei.

The third visit was honest. I had not used. I had not used since the last time I visited May 24, 1996. I had made it seven days without drug use. I circled the date on the calendar with black sharpie, permanent. I continued to refer to it, for weeks, months, years. I still hold the date close, but I did finally throw away the calendar with the date marked. I made the choice and made it every day. Every single day. From January to May, my life and Ashlei's was nearly ruined. I am lucky my addiction was short-lived. It was five months, and I could have lost custodial rights. I could have died. Ashlei could have gotten hurt. I lost four pant sizes. I increased my debt. But I lived. Ashlei got a sober mom. One day, one choice at a time.

The Christian drug counselor urged me to turn to the church. Matt's family had always been active in the church, and the advice for addicts is to fill the void left behind with something positive, and often the church is a lifeline. A religious practice is far healthier than drug use. The counselor encouraged me to get married to Matt. We did have a child together, after all. Matt never got clean. His drug use did decrease when I got sober, but he never stopped. We got married in July. Mom tried to talk me out of it. As we got ready in the bathroom before the ceremony, she looked at me pleadingly. "Hope, you don't have to do this." She hugged me tight. "The car is right out there." She pointed to the back door of the church. "Don't do this. Let's get out of here. You can change your life right now. Today."

I didn't listen.

THE CANDLESTICK IN
THE LIVING ROOM

I graduated from college in December 1996, only one semester longer than planned. Not too bad given the work commitments and challenges I created for myself. My final semester was two classes, organic 2, which I had to retake from the semester I was pregnant, and an expository writing class. My last day of class was the organic 2 final. I took the test and walked over to Mom's house on Lincoln. We celebrated by drinking Freixenet Brut in the matte black bottle. I still have the bottle. I passed the final, the class, and now was a newly minted college graduate. Success! It was a considerable milestone achieved.

The best course I took in college, and I recommend to any student, was a career development course. I took it in spring semester (yes, during the throes of my addiction cycle). We wrote resumés, applied for jobs, and conducted mock and real interviews. I interviewed with three companies that spring, one of which was Procter and Gamble in Cincinnati. The interview went well, and they offered me a job. I could not accept the offer because I had to finish the last semester. Plus, I was not sure if a move to Cincinnati was wise. Our families were in Bloomington, and they helped a lot with Ashlei. The job with P&G was not to be.

With a BS in biology in hand, I went on a scattershot job search; there was no internet or electronic applications in the mid-1990s. I applied everywhere, the old-fashioned way, using the fax machine at Matt's dad's office. I sent off resumés to a pile of random places I found in the paper. Anything that was a remote fit got a resumé and a cover letter. I was not shy, nor worried, about if I was qualified. I needed a job. A profession. During my search, I worked at a temp agency during the day. Being a temp allowed me to take time off for interview(s). I worked forty hours a week at my day job and kept three nights a week at Nick's so I could pay the bills.

One of my applications was to a privately owned medical device company in town, Cook Inc. Bill Cook was well known in the area, the richest man in the state at the time, as he ran twenty-plus companies in Bloomington, with Cook Inc. as the largest and most profitable of these companies. Bill had started the company in his garage with his wife. I interviewed and got the job.

The position was in QC Stents on the manufacturing line and paid a little less than $13,000 a year, but the benefits were phenomenal, and it was the first time we had insurance. On Medicaid while pregnant with Ashlei, we were also recipients of the Special Supplemental Nutrition Program for Women, Infants, and Children (WIC) for the first year of her life. Although WIC is helpful, paying for groceries with a voucher is humiliating and difficult, with all the stipulations on what's covered. The line stops, and the people behind you stare impatiently. The shame of incidents like these are something you never really forget. When I hear someone offhandedly say they are "broke" or "poor," I know they have never actually been poor. Being poor feels shameful, and you'd never announce it. Poor people don't say they are poor.

I had been without insurance since Mom stopped working at the dentist office when I was ten. Cook was my first job with health insurance. Although the pay was low—I had made more at KFC when I was in high school—the job fit into a larger plan, and having medical benefits was a boon. I made more money at Nick's in twenty-seven hours a week than the forty hours at Cook, but there is no upward movement as a waitress. I'd be making the same amount in ten years as a server; it was a job, not a career. Waitressing served me well those years. In fact, if not for a generous customer, I wouldn't have had an interview suit.

One crazy busy game day, I had a large table of alums who were having an excellent time. One gentleman asked me if I was going to school, and I told him I was about to graduate. He asked what I did with my tip money. I replied I was saving up for a suit to wear to interviews. Their bill was about $140, and he handed me an extra $100 bill as a tip. I gave him a chance to take it back, in case it was an accident or if he was going to have second thoughts. He said, "Keep it. Promise to get an interview suit with the money."

A $100 tip! I felt so lucky. I took my $100 to LS Ayres department store the next day. This shopping trip was luxurious and fancy, netting two suits, one blue and one red. They were early 1990s styling, which looked a lot like old 80s gear, with big shoulder pads. The suits were pretty ugly and ridiculous, but I got plenty of use out of them, especially the red one because I could use it for Christmas events. I spent that $100 well.

Now out of college and in a career job, I was launched. It felt like success. I was not making good money though. Was this success? Hope was definitely on the horizon, professionally speaking. At home, not so much. Matt and I, now newly married, were not growing closer. I still was getting my "training" at home, cleaning the house the way he wanted, improving my culinary skills, and earning my keep. The list always grew and included: the cans in the cabinet all had to be facing outward and in order, the kitchen floor must be swept after each meal and mopped on Saturdays, clean laundry could not be folded and left on the washer/dryer or in the basket, all laundry had to be put away immediately, socks had to be tuck-rolled, toes tucked in, but not a ball, more like a flat tube, and no one could ever see dirty clothes. Dirty clothes were to be hidden in a hamper in the closets, which must remain firmly shut.

I paid the rent, car payments, and utilities, and Matt was to pay for groceries. We had a stint where Matt wrote a bunch of bad checks and went to jail (my mom bailed him out). We couldn't get checking accounts at the bank. I had to pay bills by getting money orders at the grungy Village Pantry, with a small wad of cash. Embarrassing. Yet another shameful poor person activity. After a three-year waiting period, I opened a checking account in my name only. We had to keep everything separate because he was so bad with money and spent it on nothing (or drugs). I hid the box of checks at his mom's house after he stole several and forged my name to get cash.

Matt's daily meth use was gone, but he was getting high, drinking too much, and splurging on the occasional weekend of cocaine, when he could afford it. He tried his hand at selling pot but was not good at it. He smoked too much of his inventory and would give the pot away to his friends instead of selling it. His moods were volatile, yet predictable, with the drug use of choice. I knew what he had taken, or not, just by the sound of his voice. All enablers, all spouses of addicts, can read their partners.

If Matt had done coke, his voice was syrupy and sweet. He was super nice and attentive when he got home while on cocaine. It was the next day, the coming down, which led to an emotional disaster, fighting and screaming. On these days, I took Ashlei to my mom's or his mom's, or we went to play in the park. Smoking pot did not induce the highs or lows, not super nice, but not the raging mean-guy either. Different types of alcohol gave rise to different behaviors from Matt. If he was liquored up, it was violence and anger. Thrashing around the house complaining about me and my laziness, my stupidity, and how fat I was. If it was beer, he was chill, loving, and snuggly. I, the queen enabler, was adept at moving around the edges of his moods.

We had moved again, to a decent neighborhood filled with retirees, one of the few young families who lived there, and probably the only unit with violent episodes and the cops coming out with some frequency. Before I would call the cops, I called the second (or first, depending on how you look at it) enabler, Wanda, and my in-laws would come over and save the day.

Matt's Crown Royal binges were particularly sucky. Thursday or Friday nights, I could expect a throwdown. I'd send Ashlei off to Mom's house to try to protect her from the battle that was sure to ensue. One Friday night after working forty hours at Cook and eight hours at Nick's, I was not surprised to see Matt wasn't home, even though it was two-thirty in the morning. I pulled in and was careful to park correctly. I was careful to do everything correctly.

This night I hurried up, wanting to get into bed and feign being asleep by the time he got home. Maybe he wouldn't wake me up for an argument, or at least it was less likely. Taking a quick shower to get the grease and smoke smell of Nick's off me, the hot water beat my skull and helped me start to relax. Massaging the shampoo into my scalp, I heard a noise.

Shit. Is he home already?

Scrubbing faster, I rinsed the suds and stuck my face out of the curtain to listen. I didn't see or hear anything. Then the front door slammed, and he must have bounded up the stairs because in an instant the bathroom door burst open.

"Hey, Hope!" Matt boomed into the bathroom. "Whatcha doing?"

"Hey hon, just taking a shower."

"Yeah, right. Must be nice."

I did not take the bait. I did not respond.

"Are you not talking to me?" Matt flipped open the curtain as I raced to rinse off. The water bounced off me and onto the floor and his clothes. I pressed my lips together and frowned.

"Are you too good for me now?" He slurred over the

whiskey scent. "Ms. Biology? Ms. College Degree. You think you are so smart."

I turned off the shower and reached over and lifted the towel off the hook. As I patted my face dry, I said quietly, "I do not want to fight. And you know I do not think I am better than you."

"WHAT? What did you say?"

Wrapping the towel around my body, I repeated, "You know I don't think I'm better than you."

"Whatever, I know you do. Everyone knows you do." Matt seized my shoulders and gave me a push. I slipped sideways, but kept upright in the wet tub. "But we know. We know better, don't we?" He laughed. "We know how stupid you really are. You have no common sense! How you feel so pink!" He mocked me. "Ha! I feel so pink!" He shouted as he spun on his heel and crashed out of the bathroom.

I stepped out of the shower, thankful for not having to fight naked, again. I hadn't felt "pink" in a very long time. Scooping up the bundle of stinky clothes, I padded to the bedroom and could hear him rummaging in the kitchen. *Shit, what is he looking for?* Dishes crashed in the sink. I shoved the pile into the hamper and made sure I closed the closet door. My pajamas were tucked under my pillow on the far side of the bed, and I hurried to get them on.

"Hope!" Matt screamed. "Get the fuck down here right now!"

I slid on the pj pants and T-shirt. "What is it?" I yelled in return. I did not want to go down there. I felt safer in my room. If I could just get into bed, he might let it pass.

"Get down here! You fucking slob!"

I delayed. I considered. *Shit. If I don't go down there, he will run up here and push me down and probably wrestle me around. If I do go down, then there are more weapons in the kitchen. More things that can be thrown. Fuck. If I do go down, maybe I can talk him off the ledge. Tell him he is right and get to bed.*

"Okay, give me a sec." I tried to buy time knowing I can't take too long. I hoped a few seconds might help calm him. I went back to the bathroom and pulled a brush through my hair. It could be used as an implement, a weapon if needed; I kept it in hand. I plodded down the stairs while running the brush through my hair.

Matt stood at the entrance of the narrow kitchen, a strange, small smile played across his face.

"What's up? What's wrong?" I asked.

"You know what's up, Ms. Smartypants! Oh, that's right! You have no common sense!"

I said nothing.

"Have you seen what's in the sink? Did you leave it there on purpose?"

My mind flipped back to the morning. I had left for work at 6:30 a.m., dropped off Ashlei, worked all day, then went straight to Nick's. I could not remember the sink. Had I left dishes? I knew the sink had to be emptied. We could not go to bed with any dishes in the sink. The sink had to be cleaned and dried.

"This fucking pan has been soaking in there all day! Probably all night too. You are such a fucking slob. So disgusting. When are you going to get it right?" He threw his glass into the sink. It shattered, splashing shards into the air. "Is it too much to ask to wash a pan?"

I still said nothing.

"Has the dishwasher been emptied?" Matt bellowed as he flung the door open. "Nope! Is it too much to ask to empty a dishwasher?" He slammed the door shut.

"Look, Matt," I started. "I'm sorry. I've been at work all day. I just got home. I will do it now." I tried to move past him to clean the pan and empty the dishwasher. Of course, it never occurred to him that he could wash the pan. *Is it too much to ask for you to do the dishes?* I thought, but didn't dare say out loud.

"Fuck it!" He backed me up into the living room. "You were probably flirting all night with the guys at Nick's anyway. Probably looking for a boyfriend there." Little shoves. Not too much violence yet.

"Fuck, Matt." I stayed quiet, almost whispering. "Why don't you go to bed and sleep this off? I will take care of the kitchen."

He held me tight, pinning my arms to my side.

"Are you serious? Go to bed? I am going to fuck you, bitch!" He looked triumphant, daring. "Get me some! This is why we are married, right?"

I shook myself free.

"Look, Matt, I'll clean the kitchen," I replied in a small voice. "Why don't you go take a shower, then we can have sex. You smell like Crown Royal." I turned my back to him and walked toward the sink. The move was calculated. Sometimes it was better to give him my back because it disarmed him; others times it made him angrier. There wasn't much to fight about. The infraction was small. The soaking pan and the filled dishwasher. Something bigger might be a bigger fight.

"Nah, you aren't going to get away that easy. Damn, how stupid do you think I am?" He pushed me from behind, and I stumbled forward.

Whoosh. A sluicing of the air whisked next to my ear. Something sailed past me. *Thud. Bounce.*

A heavy, eight-inch brass candlestick thudded and dented the chicken coop coffee table. The candlestick rolled off and bumbled onto the carpeted floor.

I stared at it. I turned around and faced him. My lips quivered. My eyes wet with fear.

"What, Matt? What do you want?"

Snort. He lifted his chin and blinked at me. Pursed his lips, thoughtful.

What's he thinking? Does he want to take it up a notch? Am I contrite enough? Is he going to rape me now? Or go shower?

"Do you feel 'so pink' now?" he said, condescendingly. "Too bad that didn't hit your head." He walked out of the room and pounded upstairs. "Maybe it would have knocked some sense into you."

I looked at the candlestick on the ground and the divot in the table. My tears were quiet, silent like me. Small. I heard the shower turn on. I cleaned the pan. Washed and dried the sink. I put the pan and the dishes from the dishwasher away. *Maybe it is me. I must be doing something wrong. Why is he so mad about the pan? About the dishwasher? I will have to get better.*

I can do better.

Flash Forward: C202

The conference room is full. The men at the U-shaped table are all from corporate, and they give their complete attention to each successive presenter. They seemed especially interested in the business development activities presented earlier this morning. Dave is at the lectern in the front of the room, reciting the production rates for the site. I'm up next, patiently and eagerly waiting my turn, the single female in the room. These improvement metrics are impressive, and I'm excited to present them today.

My white blouse is tucked neatly into a striped pencil skirt. I am ready. More than ready. I know these numbers cold, and they are fantastic.

Dave closes his discussion and introduces my update. "Hope is going to share some of the continuous improvement activities we have been doing." He dips his chin in my direction. "Hope." He shuffles his papers together and takes his seat. I move to the front of the room.

The audience before me is the president of the business unit and his entourage of important folks. This presentation is a "big deal," and I should be nervous. I'm not. I'm early enough into my career that I do not overthink it, and I charge forward without being anxious.

"Good morning, gentlemen," I start. "I'm delighted to communicate these details with you today. We have been doing some great work, and the team is delivering on these improvement targets." I provide our numbers. I'm energetic and probably seem a bit undisciplined to these orderly men. It is rare anyone in corporate gets excited, or "passionate" in corporate-speak, but I am! I am excited. These numbers rock!

The enthusiasm is contagious. The execs in the room ask lots of questions, are engaged, and seem excited too. They want to know more. They want to hear more. They want to know how we are getting it done. A gentleman on the left side of the large, horseshoe-shaped table leans forward to get my attention and ask a question.

"Hi, Hope. I'm Brad Mueller. I've been told about the work you have been doing here. Can you tell me how you got this project initiated?"

I answer him while making a note to myself. *I need to meet that guy.* I'm in continuous improvement, and he has some corporate influence for the site in this area. Brad Mueller is someone I need to know.

The energy level rises in the room with the lively discussion. The business unit president slides both his hands along the desk in a wide-open gesture and says, "Tell me more, Hope! This is terrific!" Professional men rarely get this enthusiastic.

And I do. I'm flying high, and I overflow with information. When my time is done, I attempt to calm the room down before I leave. It is fair to say the presentation went well.

As I walk back to my office, I smile broadly, feeling great about how it went, and I remind myself that I need to meet Brad Mueller.

I unload the armful of folders onto my desk and perch on the edge of my seat. *How am I going to meet him?* He's going to be stuck in the conference room the rest of the day. I glance at my watch. They have been at it for hours, through lunch, and one more person is presenting after me. If I time it right, I might be able to catch him during the break.

I do a quick email check to fill the time. Nothing that cannot wait. I don't want to mill around outside the meeting room door; that will look desperate, so I burn a few more minutes then walk to conference room C202.

There is a bathroom down in the area near the conference room; maybe I can slip in there and buy some time. I turn the corner and look down to the end of the hall. The door to the conference room is closed. *Shit.* They must still be in there. I decide to walk by and casually peek in and see if Ben, the guy who went after me, is still presenting.

As I proceed down the hall, Brad comes out of the men's room. A few feet in front of me! Perfect timing.

He glances in my direction, sees me, and stops.

"Hi." I walk up to him and extend my right hand. "I'm Hope."

"Yes!" he reciprocates. "You are." We shake hands. Firm, good eye contact, and an easy smile. Blue eyes. "I'm Brad Mueller. It sounds like we have some work we can do together."

"I was thinking the same thing."

We move our conversation to the edge of the hall and a nearby window. We lean against the window well and have a quick conversation. Brad and I shake hands again with a commitment to discuss how to partner on our local and corporate continuous improvement efforts together.

Nice. I need to have him on my side and help me get projects sponsored, supported, funded, and pulled-through as needed. *Very nice.*

We start working together, and I can't ever remember his title, which he gives me a hard time about. I have never been good at remembering titles; I try to treat everyone equally important regardless of status or position. We have several phone calls and, the next time he visits our site, I loan him my office. I hang up his business card on my bulletin board so I will remember his title. Maybe, too, I like seeing his name. I do not admit it to myself at our first meeting, or the next, but my actions show I like him.

I like Brad's side of the story too. He confesses he wanted to marry me thirty seconds into my presentation. He also says I asked him out first. That is not how I remember it. He asked me out three times, sure it was only to lunch. Twice I said no because I had no childcare. The third time, a dinner appointment, I had said yes, then I had to cancel at the last minute. I felt bad about cancelling and asked him to go to an opera with me next time he was to be in town. He couldn't go. Brad claims he doesn't remember the first three times he asked me out; he only remembers me inviting him to the opera.

It doesn't matter. We are together now. A work partnership led to a life partnership. Now the who-asked-who-out-first is a fun bit of banter we play. And for the record, we have never been to the opera (and he asked me out first).

IGNORANCE ON FIRE

Days on the line at Cook Inc. were boring. When I got home from work, I cried from the boredom. Eight hours a day quality controlling 50-100 pieces. Manual, visual, checking and measuring. No mental challenge. Books on tape saved my sanity. Then I was temporarily assigned to the research and development (R&D) organization, and it was a total blast. I worked on projects creating new medical devices, and it was fabulous.

After being in the R&D group for a few weeks, I had to go back to the line. We launched the first stent into the market, and we worked nonstop to keep up with demand with loads of mandatory overtime. The hours were crazy, working seven days a week at Cook and waitressing at nights. Demand started to level off, and I was asked to move into the R&D group permanently because I was degreed. I jumped at the chance. There was a problem, though, which I did not know about until later. The problem was no one wanted to work with me. The R&D teams all thought I was too "strong," too bossy. I acted like I knew everything. And I was green. I had no idea about anything. How could I pretend I knew about catheters and introducers, melt properties and forming tech?

There were five teams, and finally one, with Scott and Kim, were willing to take me on board. Kim was the one who told me none of the teams wanted to work with me and why. I was surprised. I had no idea people saw me this way. She said they called me a "bulldozer." I thought I was being eager, helpful, and smart. I thought I was providing support and energy to move projects forward. The awareness of how I was being perceived led me to a foundational lesson in my career.

David, my boss, shared with me Stephen Covey's book *Seven Habits of Highly Effective People*. He discussed the concept of relationship accounts and how not to be perceived as a "bulldozer." Before sharing ideas and working with people, I had to build a relationship account. You must make deposits before making withdrawals. This analogy resonated with me, and I clung to its concepts and put them into action at work. The fast-friend approach I took as a kid did not work in the corporate setting, and really had stopped working in middle school. People do not expect you to be full-on day one. You need to build relationships. I am glad I got this lesson early, and I have been using the approach to increasing success since that day. Twenty years into my career, I do a decent job at cultivating positive relationships with colleagues, and it serves a foundation for productive, positive teamwork.

My time at work was a haven, and I flourished. I worked hard and learned how to get along with people in a real way. I valued my coworkers tremendously, and I learned how to show it. Working in R&D was fascinating. Kim and Scott were great teachers and endlessly patient with my eager ass. The corporate phrase for this type of behavior is "Ignorance on Fire." That was me! Highly willing and enthusiastic without any knowledge. I did not yet have the experience or capability to support such excitement. Cook, a privately held company, was not heavy on leadership training, and they did not know what to call me or barely knew what to do with me. Thankfully, I found people who were patient, kind, and willing to train me to calm the fuck down.

Although I enjoyed the work, the pay was paltry. Heading into year two, I continued the second job at Nick's. Cook had another company across the street, a pharmaceutical manufacturing facility, with an open position for a microbiologist. I had a biology degree and had taken microbiology in college. I loved the micro class, and I enjoyed the lab portion even more. We once had to streak our own urine, and my lab partner's plate grew with *Staph aureus*, which I found hilarious. My plate was clean, which is right because unless you have a bladder infection, urine is sterile. Our final for the class was to identify three unknown organisms. So fun! I thought being a microbiologist would be a good fit, and it was a better-paying job.

I applied, interviewed, and accepted the job at Cook Pharma Solutions in the micro laboratory. I was nervous though. *Would I be able to do this job? Was I smart enough?* I plunged forward. The $27,000 annual salary felt like I was the richest person ever. I was able to quit my waitressing job and took my student loans out of deferment. Here we go! Holy shit! I've made it!

Mom gave me the greatest Christmas gift that year. She had my degree framed. I opened the framed certificate and cried. I was happy and proud. The salaried position meant I had made it, and a degree had worth and meaning. Working hourly for minimal pay for eighteen months after I graduated, it was hard to see the value in the degree, but here, here it was. I was a microbiologist. I was making the student loan payments, and I was salaried. I was starting a career, for real. And though I never said it out loud, I was feeling a little pink.

The work was simple. It was a QC lab after all, repetitive work, collecting and testing samples. I was not developing the cure for cancer. This was a time of explosive education and growth for me. The microbiology teams in pharma test the product and take care of the facility and utilities—all of the water systems, air systems, compressed gas systems, air exchange rates, materials of construction, zones of sampling, different tests for each different product and facility measure. I could go on and on. I loved it. It was incredible and eye opening, exciting and challenging. I excelled. I learned as much as I possibly could, did anything they let me, and mastered the activities in the laboratory. Work was joy.

When a colleague quit and went to Eli Lilly, I gave her my resumé, in case they might be hiring. She called me a few months later and said there was an opening. I applied to an environmental monitoring microbiologist position. They offered me the job at $45,000 and a $10,000 signing bonus. Holy shit, again. I was literally the richest person on the planet.

I was smart. I was valued. I was respected.

Until I went home.

PI

3:14 a.m.

The contractions tighten my belly. I open my eyes and wait. *This hurts.* The muscles scrunch harder. My swollen belly is a rock. I rub the top of my baby bump, smoothing out the pain. This is our second baby, albeit almost seven years apart, and I have been in latent labor for three weeks. The due date is seven days out, and I'm already at three centimeters.

Even pregnant, I have not missed a beat working in the microbiology lab, and it got interesting having contractions at work for the past weeks. I'd stop midstride and wait for the clench to pass. I breathed a little more specifically, and everyone in the room paused with me. They looked horrified that the baby was coming. We had a sterility suite, and we'd planned a labor and delivery in that room. It's a game we played to lighten the mood. None of us, least of all me, wanted to deliver a baby at work.

This contraction was different. I knew it at that moment, 3:14 a.m.—my baby would join the world that day. A few months prior to this pregnancy, I had a miscarriage at six weeks. I was surprised at how crushed and emotional I was. The doctor had to do a dilation and curettage (D&C), a similar procedure to an abortion. I was worried. *Had the abortion all those years ago messed up my uterus? Did it damage me in some way? Was there something wrong? Was I a woman who could still carry, deliver, and nurture a baby?*

The inability, or so I thought, to have a baby slammed into the concept of who I was as a woman. I must be able to bear a child. I am a woman. My wide hips and breasts are proof of my purpose in this world. I tried to forgive myself. I tried to convince myself everything was fine, that it was not my fault. Having the miscarriage flipped being able to get pregnant into a goal, a requirement for me, and how I defined who I was as a female. The real question is, *Why was I having another child while in this unhealthy relationship?* It was simple—I wanted Ashlei to have a sibling, someone to commiserate with after I died. The answer is unsatisfactory, with the marriage I was in; looking at the decision now, it was far from logical. The psychosis of abuse victims includes rationalizing our lives and playing like everything is fine.

A few months after the miscarriage, I am pregnant again. And today is the day. I know it at 3:14 a.m. *I am having this baby today.*

The pregnancy had been horrible—to be accurate, life with Matt was horrible, not the pregnancy. A few months into the pregnancy, I went with Katy to Vermont to attend Jamaica's wedding. Her mountaintop ceremony was beautiful. Meanwhile, a friend of Katy's came to town for a high school reunion and hung out with Matt while we were gone. I thought nothing of it. Whatever, yeah sure, take him to the reunion, have fun. I didn't give a second thought about this woman, Bridgette, and Matt going to the reunion together.

I had my assumptions about Matt though. Matt, now an EMT, worked at a firehouse, twenty-four-hour shifts, for a few days on and a few days off. I had found condoms in his bag. Strange numbers on his beeper. Scraps of scrawled love notes in his pockets. So yeah. He was probably cheating on me. Funny how I thought "probably." Funny how people lie to themselves. Somehow, I thought I deserved it. I deserved to be cheated on. Matt never admitted anything, even when faced with the evidence. He brushed it off. He lied. I knew he lied. We both knew; we both pretended to not know and moved on. Our life together was merely transactional.

When Katy and I returned from the weekend wedding, Bridgette was sitting on my couch. She pulled a long black hair off the cushion and told me, "Sorry if you find my hair everywhere." I didn't blink. I trusted her. I did not trust

Matt. I trusted her because of her connection with Katy. What kind of person fucks her pregnant friend's husband?

Weeks later, Matt came to me. I was putting away laundry in Ashlei's room.

"Hopey, I got to tell you something."

"Huh?" I faced him and kept folding her little shirts.

"Fuck. I don't know where to start."

I stopped mid-fold and looked at him. He looked strange, almost sad.

"Look, you gotta help me." He sat down on Ashlei's bed.

"Okaaaaay?" I perched on the edge of the bed.

"Bridgette called. Has been calling." He shrugged. "I don't know what is going on. She is being crazy."

"What? You mean Katy's friend, Bridgette? The one you went to the reunion with?"

"Yeah. She is crazy, Hope. You are going to have to talk to her."

"Me? What?" I rubbed my belly. "Why? Did you fuck her? Is she pregnant too?" I deadpanned.

"No! We hung out the whole weekend when you were gone. Now she's being crazy." He paused. "We've been talking. A lot. Well, off and on for the past couple of weeks." He looked at me, befuddled.

"Just tell me."

"I don't know, Hope. She is saying she loves me. She wants to move back here from California to be with me."

"Ha," I snorted. "Matt, you have to have this wrong. Why would she want to be with you? You are married. You have one kid and another on the way." I stood up and started folding the clothes again. "Matt, you have it wrong."

Matt had always been able to charm people, and women considered him attractive. He convinced people what a great guy he was. Eventually, folks would see through his charade. This woman had a fun weekend with him and now wants to move home from California to be with him? I thought it was funny. I figured he must be misunderstanding her. No way she wanted to move here to be with my husband.

"Hope, she says she loves me and wants to be with me."

"But why? Have you been telling her you love her too?"

"I don't know. Well, maybe. I mean yeah. Probably. I don't know. You have to call her. You have to tell her I can't be with her."

Shit. I was not laughing now. Here was the first time Matt had admitted, sort of, to anything. He was acting like a panicked sixth-grader with too many girlfriends. We were adults, yet he was asking me—his wife—to bail him out of a tangle with a girlfriend. Once I had to shoo a raccoon out of the garage for him, and now I had to shoo this woman out of our life. This was too much. This was my life. Matt made messes, and I cleaned them up.

"Hope, look, I did not mean for it to get so serious." His eyes darted around. "It was just the weekend of fun. You said I could go to the reunion with her. Fuck. You have to talk to her. You have to tell her we can't be together."

I sat back down, my heart skipping beats and the baby kicking my tummy inside. I was not sad, barely mad, more resigned. Ugh. *This is so fucked up.*

"She says she wants to move here to be with me. What are you going to do?"

"Me?! What am I going to do?? Fuck, Matt! What are YOU going to do?" I took a breath, glanced at the tree outside of Ashlei's window, turned to face him and asked, "Do you want to be with her?"

"NO! No, no. Why would I be telling you this if I wanted to be with her?" He paused and was looking for an escape. "You have to tell her she can't be with me."

"Are you really asking me to break up with your girlfriend?" I shook my head. Fuck. I was annoyed. Frustrated. Numb. What was wrong with me? What was wrong with this whole picture? There was no love here. What was the deal with Matt? It was maintenance. I was the enabler. I was the fixer. Matt, for all his bravado, leaned on me to manage his life. And I stayed. I was now pregnant with our second baby, and I stayed. What the hell was wrong with me? I was the one who had to fix things. Now I was supposed to fix this? *Fuck. Are you kidding me?*

I called her while I sat on Ashlei's bed, my swollen belly resting on my lap. Matt sat next to me. I got sad when I heard her voice. It was her voice and her non-answers that broke through to my emotions. *How had my life gotten so messed up?* She didn't admit to having sex with him, which was not really the point. I felt nothing for Matt. I told her he was my husband, the man with whom I had a child and was pregnant with another. I tried to suss out a plan. "Do you want to move here to be with him?" There was some sort of affirmative. I can't remember exactly how the conversation went. I remember a ringing in my ears and a heavy sorrow weighing on me. *What kind of life was I living? What in the hell was wrong with me?* My baby kicked me back into the moment. I hung up the phone.

Time went by, and this woman was never mentioned again. I guess they broke up. I should have told her to come. I should have let her take him on. I should have walked away from Matt that afternoon.

The weeks after the call were much more painful for me. I was tangled up in cycles of analysis on why I still stayed. I pondered my options, who I was, and how was I going to live. I was a few short months, weeks, from having a baby. The evolutionary mind sinks to low levels, or at least mine did. I did not want to be alone in the delivery room. I did not want to be an unwed pregnant mother, again. I had already been that when I had Ashlei. We were not married when Ashlei was born. We were now. We went to church, and the church expected us to stay married. I had a distorted sense of what it meant to be a good wife. The wife was the caretaker. The wife makes sure the family works. The wife holds it all together. I slipped into self-loathing.

I deserve this.

That's what I told myself. It's okay if he sleeps with other women. I was fat. I was pregnant. I was a stupid slob, right? I should be okay with him sleeping with other women occasionally. I knew he had condoms and was gone all the time. I knew what was going on. It was okay. I didn't deserve differently anyway. Maybe it was my fault. It must be my fault. I must be defective. Maybe I was pushing him away. I was not "in love" with him. I took care of him and our family and our household. I tolerated, enabled, and fixed him, but I was not in love. I have no idea what he felt for me.

I was busy with a miracle growing in my body, and I worried about what the stress hormones were doing to the baby. I had to let it go and move on. I could stay strong. I could handle it. I could handle anything.
3:14 a.m.

The contractions continue. I get up and putter around the house until Matt and Ashlei wake up. "We are having the baby today," I declare.

I call into work. Matt calls into work. I have Ashlei stay home from school. Mom comes over. I plan to stay home as long as possible before going to the hospital.

We have a jigsaw puzzle working on the kitchen table

and, while my contractions pace through, I work the puzzle. As the contractions grow in intensity and frequency, Mom gets nervous. "Hopey, we need to get to the hospital."

"I am going to finish this puzzle, then we will go."

The discomfort is peaking, and I know we should go soon. I put the last puzzle piece into place.

"Okay! We can go!" I stand up, and my water breaks. I have waited too long. The pains come on fast and furious. I change my leggings, and we hurry to the car. Although the hospital is a short seven-minute drive from our house, it feels like a lifetime. I think I'm going to have the baby in the car.

Matt pulls into the hospital parking garage; the parking ticket says 2:46 p.m. Olivia Storm arrives at 3:14 p.m. My little Pi life.

SWEET FIRE PICKLES

The car radio saved me. You see, it died.

Eli Lilly was on the south side of Indianapolis, a sixty-minute drive door-to-door, the first time I had to commute more than fifteen minutes to work. The job was great. I developed immensely during my years there. I discovered my capacity and interest in work, I began to put in ten-to-twelve-hour days, and loved it. I was leading and partnering with people. I was responsible for massive projects that forced rapid growth and development. I gained deep knowledge in the pharmaceutical industry and specifically environmental monitoring. All of the people I worked with had been at Lilly for ten-fifteen-twenty-plus years. I was the most junior member of the team, and I quickly became the person people came to for answers, guidance, and decisions. People knew I was someone who could get things done, make sure actions were achieved, and projects were completed on time. Officially I was no one's boss, but

I was responsible for scheduling and coordinating the lab's activities. I was intelligent, efficient, and trusted at work. And no one called me a bulldozer. Or a fat stupid slob.

I had been at Lilly for several months when the car radio died. No morning talk radio, no sound, no music, nothing to distract me while I commuted to and from work. The death of the noise helped me gain perspective of my life. There was no extra money to replace or repair the radio, so the quiet was mine to manage. The first few days of driving in the dark silence were unnerving. What can a person do with 120 minutes of quiet reflective time a day? Plenty. The sixty minutes of the morning drive were filled with planning for the oncoming workday. I was wonderfully busy and had several complex projects. This time was useful in sorting my plans and actions for the days and weeks ahead. I probably owe some measure of accomplishment at Lilly to the broken radio.

The drive home increasingly became reflective. I planned for home activities, and then I spent time considering my life. I was in an unhealthy marriage, with a drug addict husband. No matter how great the day at work was, when I got home, I was fat, a slob, and stupid—never good enough.

Matt's surveillance and expectations for me never paused. I was a pig if I left a closet door open or didn't shut a dresser drawer all the way. My dishwashing was never good enough, neither was my housekeeping. The baseboards needed wiping each week, and I got down on my hands and knees, scraping the edges of the carpet near the baseboard to remove the grey dust that settled there. Matt preferred to have the carpet combed. I don't know if it was OCD or too many lines of coke in the afternoon. He had a specific wide-toothed hair comb he used to smooth the edges of the carpet. I was expected to take care of everything else. If things were not clean enough or straight enough or fast enough, a rage might flare. If all was not up to par, dishes got destroyed, furniture got tossed, and I was left to clean the aftermath. I lost one of my grandma's bowls to a not-clean-enough rageful fit, and I loved that bowl.

In addition to my slovenliness, my cooking was not good enough either. Dinner often came with the regular side dish of a verbal beat down. My food was passable at best. Dinner was either too dry or too bland or served with, *Fuck, bitch, why are you such a horrible cook?*

I picked at my food and did not eat too much because I was "fat."

"Why do you weigh so much? Your jeans are bigger than mine! When are you going to lose some weight?"

The biggest dichotomy between work and home was my "stupidity." Matt was confident of how stupid I was. He thought that although I might be "book smart," I had no common sense. I purportedly did not even know how to cross the street. I did not know "how the world worked." I was to sit back and watch the "master." The phrase "I feel so pink" commonly got thrown in my face. Somewhere inside I knew this to be false. Not until the silence in the car did I have the opportunity to evaluate and dissect the truth of my intelligence, healthfulness, or happiness, or lack thereof.

At work, I was brilliant, dynamic, and sought out for advice. At home, I was a stupid waste of a human.

The drive to work was uplifting, exciting, and I was eager to get to work. The drive home was the opposite. After picking up the girls, I drove slower and slower to extend the time before we walked in the door. I did not want to return to being a dumb slob. I had been an awesome contributor all day. I was moving from a trusted and respected environment to a home where I was ridiculed and mocked.

As the months proceeded with no sound to fill the air and mind during the alone time in the car, the difference drew in sharper relief. I was wonderful at work and useless at home.

Both could not be true. I must be a little smart? A little awesome? I mean all the other people in my life, except my husband, believed and told me so. As this became clearer, I gravitated towards who I was at work. I was smart. I was capable. I was amazing. *Who was Matt to psychologically beat me with his version of the truth?*

The car radio was silent for nine months. During that gestation time, I had two hours a day to consider life. It was during these 32,400 minutes of solitude I grew stronger. I knew I could not stay with Matt. I had to free myself and my girls from this toxic, unhappy homelife. I didn't just walk in and announce it, but the idea formed, and I knew what I had to do.

Once I saw this truth, I could not unsee it. Each small comment Matt made, every utterance of my failures, stood out and was noticed. His cutting remarks were so common and regular they used to float over me, barely registering how I was belittled and made small. It was our norm. Now each phrase from his lips became a loud beacon of light shouting at me.

Nevertheless, I was lax. I was slow to act. And most upsetting, I didn't realize he was doing the same thing to Ashlei.

Matt's demeaning of our daughter was not as frequent as his incessant berating of me, but it was often enough to be noticed by friends and family. Of course, no one said anything to him. This was common in our relationship; same as at work, people knew who got things done and took care of our family. Even his buddies approached me to resolve their business deals with him that went wrong. If he did not pay someone for something, either work related or drugs, his friends often asked me to take care of it. More than once I stood at the door explaining to someone how Matt was home but he would not talk to them, and they had to clear off my porch. This was different. Family and friends were approaching me because they were concerned about Matt's treatment of Ashlei.

"You see how he is treating Ashlei?" Wanda asked.

"What do you mean?"

"Honey, how do you not see it? He is on her all the time."

I had not acknowledged it. "But he loves her," I defended. "He loves her most in this world."

"Maybe, but that doesn't make it okay for him to treat her that way. She is never good enough for anything."

I started to pay closer attention and realized Wanda was right; Matt was turning his ire onto Ashlei. She was seven and smart. And he didn't like it. I noticed his favorite refrain for chiding her was, "You are just like your mom." Or, "Girl, you better get some common sense."

Mom had a similar conversation with me, warning me how damaging Matt's behavior was to Ashlei's psyche. The whole realization came to a head when, in the same week, his two best friends talked to me about how they were concerned with the way he treated Ashlei. They were both troubled with Matt's new whipping post becoming his daughter.

I had to grasp my own fault in this situation. When I really challenged myself, I knew at some level I had noticed what was going on and in some twisted way was relieved when he took out his anger from time to time on someone else. I did not do this consciously. After months of silent time in the car, I realized this wedge of truth. When I started seeing, really seeing, how damaging his behavior and actions were, I was crushed that I had allowed Ashlei, even for a second, to be the brunt of his verbal attacks. I knew I had to ensure it never happened again.

I felt massive guilt when I realized my passive allowance of his treatment of our daughter. Guilt gets you nowhere. I now had to fight back for Ashlei. Every slight was now noted and immediately addressed. I became Ashlei's defender. I did not let a comment pass without my correction to him. He was not going to destroy my daughter. Say what he wanted about me, I could take it, but Ashlei was a child, and I was no longer going to let her be degraded by this man.

I needed to claw back myself. My first actions were to protect Ashlei.

The commentary on me continued. Any remark on Ashlei, I took the fire, protecting her.

Of course, Matt ate it up, and he gloated. "After all, Hope, you know you are a slob," he taunted. I had heard it often enough; now I was starting to know better. I took small actions to gain ground. Matt did not like it if the sponge was left in the sink. I did not purposely leave it there. I did not purposely put it away either. I did not drive home in a hurry to get dinner started; I took my time and did not worry if he would be mad. These actions helped reinforce the truth that I was a good and okay person. If there was a passing remark, I would respond in my head: *No, Matt, I actually have loads of common sense. Here are three examples from this week.*

Matt wanted me home, before he got home, either with dinner made or at least started. One day, Wanda and I went to get sweet fire pickles from a rural neighboring county store. These pickles were amazing. Wanda made the greatest snack with them: Ritz cracker, sharp white cheddar, and a sweet fire pickle.

I was driving Wanda's living-room-like maroon Cadillac, which I thought was the nicest, most expensive car ever. Now I know better. A used Cadillac in the mid-nineties was not a reflection of wealth or status; it was a reflection of age. We got lost on the back roads of Brown County. Maybe it was Jackson county; we were that lost. These were the days before GPS, and we were so far out in the boonies I doubt a GPS would have worked there anyway.

"Oh, honey," Wanda worried, "we are going to be late. Matt is going to be so upset."

"I know," I responded with a shrug while looking for the next crossroad.

"Well, you don't sound concerned."

I was months into my claw back.

"Yeah. It doesn't matter. I mean, he is always mad. It doesn't matter if I clean the house perfectly. It doesn't matter if I have dinner ready. It doesn't matter if I have paid the bills and we have a refrigerator full of groceries. He is still going to find a reason to be mad. He will still find a reason to yell."

As I talked, I realized I was getting stronger.

"It will be something," I continued. "There is always something. The sponge will be in the wrong place, the car parked too close to the garage door, or not far enough away. The food will be undercooked, dry, or not enough salt. It will be something, there always is, so we might as well enjoy our adventure. And these pickles! They are the worth the road trip. We can't hurry up anyway; we don't even know where we are!" I laughed and glanced at her.

Wanda looked surprised at my mirth but maybe, just maybe, a little relieved. My lack of anxiety allowed her to not be too anxious. We drove a little too fast, with the music a little too loud, and we laughed. It felt good to laugh.

"Aha! A road we know!" I said, as we found our way back. Now we could get home. We talked the whole way, about work and family and pickles, and I felt comfortable and happy. I noticed it too. I was going to be late, and I wasn't worried about the anger that would meet me at the door. With a case of sweet fire pickles on the floorboards behind me, and a new sweet fire burning within me, I felt empowered, and I was moving in a new direction.

INDY 500

W e walk into the house from the garage after church. Ashlei presses play on the answering machine. I'm still holding Olivia in her car carrier. The bulky seat is heavy on my forearm. The diaper bag and my purse weigh down the other side of me.

The long beep sounds. Laughter and other raucous noises emanate into the orderly living room.

"Stop. Stop." It's Matt's voice, but he is not yet talking to us. "Wait. I'm leaving a message for my wife."

"*Oooooh . . .*" giggles a female voice. "*Ssshhmmmm . . .*"

"Hey, Hope. It's me. I'm at the speedway." Matt pauses. I imagine him putting his fingers to his lips to shush his partner. "Everything is pretty quiet here. Um. No accidents." I can hear him smiling. "I'll be here the next few nights."

Click.

Taking a deep breath, I start to unburden my load. Olivia gurgles, unaware of the chaos that is our life.

Beeeeeeeeeep.

Another message fires off. Now we hear keys jangling and more laughter. "Wait! Give me those!" The phone thuds and bounces on the floor, the recording device not missing a sound.

I stand up straight, still with the diaper bag and purse on my left shoulder, and hurry to the machine to press delete. I turn back to the baby carrier and wrangle the five-point seatbelt loose and lift Olivia out, and put her to my chest.

Beeeeeeeeeep.

Matt's hiccupping messages continue. Intimate groans, a rustling of body movements, and more giggles emit from the machine. Ashlei's face contorts in a confused twitch. I take another deep breath, shifting Olivia to my hip to press delete before the scene continues.

"What was that, Mama?" Ashlei asks. "Is Daddy okay?"

Beeeeeeeeeep.

Another message. The sounds of a playful wrestling match fill our home, complete with more laughter, body rolls, and keys being tossed around. "Hey, hey . . . give me those . . . don't . . . hey . . . I think I am calling my wife. Wait, just wait . . ."

Delete.

Beeeeeeeeeeep.

The machine starts again. A moaning orgasm is being gleefully pitched for my ears. All our ears.

Delete.

Beeeeeeeeeeep.

The machine is old, and I cannot proactively delete the messages. I have to let them start to play before I can delete them. I wait and delete three more messages.

The room is hushed, the air now crisp with an emptiness and tension. I am stone. Ashlei looks like she is playing the game "Freeze" with her right hand caught open, palm in midair. Her face is scrunched up in a question. We are paused in motion, except Olivia who shoves her hand in her mouth and paws at my shirt.

The moment is clear, my mind is clear, and I decide. I am done. Those beeps fortified the decision made. It's a decision I have made a thousand times before. This time I feel relief. I know it will be done.

"Mom?" Ashlei asks, "what was that girl doing? Who was that? Who is Daddy with?"

"Baby, I don't know. It sounds like they were playing around or something." I make excuses for him, something I had been doing far too long. What else could I say? I close my arms around Olivia and turn my attention to unpacking from the morning trek.

We had been at church for Olivia's dedication ceremony.

I'd stood at the front of the 200-plus-person congregation with the other couples who'd had babies born in the previous six months. Matt was supposed to be with me. He got called into work to cover the Indianapolis 500, a legitimate reason for missing this special family occasion. When I returned to my seat, a woman next to me leaned in and asked where my husband was. That's when I realized I was the only single person at the front of the church. Not single in the not-married sense, but single-without-the-other-parent-there sense.

I had stood alone holding Olivia, in my ugly floral skirt, pink shirt, and cream cardigan. It never occurred to me that it was odd to be up there without her father. I did not think to be embarrassed or angry until several people asked about his whereabouts. Then I started to get upset because he was not there. He was never there for us.

I did not need him to stand with me and commit Olivia to anything. Truth was, I had not needed him for anything for a long time. Our marriage was a sham. The frustration of it all festered in me and followed me out of the church. I nursed the annoyance as we drove home, and it coursed through me when we entered the house.

The electronic bell tone of the answering machine popped the bubble and released me. This is the last straw in a series of a thousand straws.

A few days later Matt comes home, and I sit on the

edge of our bed waiting for him. When he walks into the bedroom, he does not greet me. He drops his bag on the bed and starts to take off his shirt.

"I want a divorce," I say quietly. I am not mad. I am not loud. It's a simple statement of fact.

Matt laughs and ignores me. "We've got plans tonight, Hope; let's get going."

He traipses to the closet to switch out his work shirt. "I want to have some fun tonight." He looks at me, but does not really see me. "I'm hungry. Let's go. Suck it up."

I watch him, and know he does not understand the depths of my commitment to this decision. I stare at the closed closet doors. He glances at me and realizes I am upset.

"Look, hon," he comes over and rests his hands on my shoulders. "We can talk about this later." He kisses the top of my head and smooths down my hair. "Let's have fun with Rusty and Linda tonight." He shoves his arms through a T-shirt and walks out to the bathroom.

I will suck it up for the evening. I am the master of the happy mask. I wipe the silent tears away with the flat of my hand and take a steadying breath. I rise from the bed and move to fix my face. I dab on some powder. No one would know I had been crying. No one ever knows.

We go out to dinner that night with Rusty and Linda. Matt acts if nothing is wrong because he does not know. To him nothing is wrong. He does not know I am done. He does not know I am serious. This is our life, this lie of joy.

The four of us sit nestled together in a small booth, with Linda complaining about Rusty all evening. As I pick at my Stromboli, Linda rants about how Rusty scratched a hubcap on her car. He had taken her car to get washed as a surprise, and the machine marred the hubcap. Linda is furious about it and will not let the matter drop. As she drinks her vodka and cranberry and laments her lot in life, all I can think is how she is ungrateful and stupid. She has no idea how good she has it. Rusty worships her.

I never say a word. I don't mention my husband's infidelity or rage. I don't mention this fucked up marriage. I stab the sweet pickles on the plate and think, *I am done.* I am done with all of this.

I am done.

FLASH FORWARD: STELLA

Brad snatches the last chip from the basket, scrapes the guacamole dish, and happily crunches the chip. I laugh as he wipes the crumbs from his chin.

This dinner is on Chris, my colleague, who had lost our bet. He bet that the Kansas Jayhawks men's basketball team would beat the Indiana Hoosiers. I took the bet, not believing IU would win but supporting them nonetheless. Indiana won, and Chris now owed us dinner. Hooray!

Brad, Chris, and I chat about work as we sip margaritas and lament our poor performing basketball teams. Beyond the hoops action, Chris has enthralled us by describing his new Tesla. The Model S is a 100 percent electric car, it can be summoned, driven on autopilot, and goes 0-60 in 3.6 seconds. Brad and I are curious and cannot get enough. The car sounds amazing. Smooth ride. Fast acceleration. With all the bells and whistles of a high-end luxury car.

Chris pays the bill, and we amble outside to view Chris's gleaming vehicle with reverent appreciation. We *ooh* and *ahh* over the chrome on black-recessed handles and the cute little electric port. No engine to look at. Chris pops open the frunk and we peer inside a small front trunk. We marvel at the beauty.

"Let's take a ride!" Chris nearly shouts.

The door handles extend as we near.

"Brad, you drive." Chris makes his way around the car to the passenger side. I swing open the back door and clamber in. I giggle with excitement and am nervous for Brad to drive.

"Okay, give me the key!"

"You don't need a key." Chris holds up a fob shaped like a Tesla (even *it* is super cool). "I have the fob. No key needed. Let's do it."

"All righty," Brad responds with awe. "Let's see what she can do." He swings open the door and climbs in, acting confident, but I can see he is edgy.

"How do I start it?" Brad asks. There is nothing. No keyhole, obviously. No push button. Nothing that indicates "start."

"It's on." Chris chortles, clearly happy to share this toy with friends. The car is totally silent. Nothing. You cannot tell it is on. There is nothing *on* about it.

"Put your foot on the brake and push this lever down to R to back out," Chris instructs.

A giant video feed from the back of the car pops up on the seventeen-inch screen.

"Wow! That's insane!"

Brad backs the sweet beast out carefully, and we exit the restaurant's parking lot.

"What is it doing? It slows down when I ease off the gas." Brad shakes his head. "I mean accelerator."

"It's the regenerative braking. When you release the accelerator, the car slows, so you don't have to use the brakes as much, and it loads energy back into the battery."

"All right, all right." Brad is easing along. It is nerve-wracking to drive someone else's expensive investment.

"Push it," Chris instructs. "It's okay, just push it."

Blast! I am thrown back into the seat. The g-force pins me to the cushions. Like a rocket, or a rollercoaster, we fly down the road. Brad takes his foot off the accelerator, and the car quickly decelerates. The thing is crazy. I roll with laughter and giddy delight, whooping and hollering in the back seat.

Brad is screaming, "Wow! Whoa! Wow!"

"That is fucking amazing! I love it! That is awesome!" I belt out between giggles. "Do it again, Brad! Do it again!" I cheer.

"That was insane." Brad lifts his hands from the wheel and stares in wonder at the car. He expertly twists us around the mall loop parking lot, alternatively slowing down then punching it, and we all get thrown back into our seats.

The car is pulsating with laughter and elated energy.

Chris turns to look at me. "Now it's your turn, Hope."

"Ahhhh. No way," I decline. "I'm too nervous. My adrenaline is through the roof!"

"Come on! You will love it!"

"Not today. I will drive her, not today though."

"All right. I will hold you to it. You will love it."

"Will love it? I already do. This is amazing." I can't stop smiling.

The car is silent as we make our way back to the restaurant lot. It makes no noise except a quiet futuristic whooshing sound when it is first accelerated. We pull in next to Brad's Ford Explorer, which up to then we thought was a great car.

I get out of the back seat and shut the door, admiring the sleek lines. "Damn. What a sensational car! Damn."

Hugs all around, thank yous exchanged, and a few more digs on the Hoosier win, then Brad and I load up into the Explorer. As I fasten my belt, still filled with the thrill of the ride, Brad looks at me and states, "We are buying that car. We are getting a Tesla."

Two years later we did.

We planned, saved, and executed. We took the day off work on the day we were scheduled to pick the car up. We drove her around all afternoon, screaming and laughing. I kept repeating, "We bought a roller coaster! We bought a roller coaster!"

Stella, our Model S, was named by our daughter Lauren. She is blue, beautiful, and makes the commute to work an absolute joy. Brad loves that this is my car. It was outrageously expensive, but as he commonly says, "You deserve it." He believes I deserve this much joy, this much luxury, this much speed. For him it is a status symbol of how far I have come. Thank you, Brad, for this gift—not just the car, but the love and pampering.

Thank you, Chris, for the test drive!

THE SLAP

At 2:47 a.m. the front door was swung open by Matt and his friend, Dan. They stomped in, uncaring about the racket they were making with the sleeping kids upstairs. I instantly realized Matt was coked up because he was being so sweet.

"Hey baby," he hummed. "What are you doing up?"

I had been getting stronger. I knew it. I felt it. Something in me was shifting. I was at the kitchen sink, filling up a glass of water, fuming.

No. No more. It is not okay to come home at 2:47 a.m. drunk and coked up. No. This must stop. He had to go.

My flat expression showed my displeasure as I pushed past him toward the living room.

"Aww, Hopey, don't be mad," Matt said with a sloppy side grin and the glassy eyes of too many lines and a few Budweisers.

"Why did you even come home?" I started in. "Fuck, Matt."

"I know. I know. But hey, I'm here." He reached for my hips for a playful sway. I slipped out of his grasp and headed for the stairs.

I had laid awake for the past three hours and twenty-seven minutes. I got tired of the book I was reading. I got tired of watching the clock. I got tired of the fact that our life was still a disaster. And I was wide awake and ready for a change.

I have the strength. Does he know it? Does he know how capable I am? What the fuck do I need this guy for anyway? I make more money than he does. The condo is in my name. He contributes nothing. I am strong. I don't need him.

"Hopey, don't be mad," Matt lolled again. "We were at Nick's. We just had a few drinks."

"Matt," I carried the water and paused at the bottom of the stairs. "I don't care where you have been. Good night." I glared at him. "And you know what? You stink," I stated. I trudged up the carpeted steps. Matt followed close behind. I could feel his body near me, and I could smell him.

"Hopey . . ."

One step.

Two steps. His breath fouled the air.

"Baby . . ."

Three steps.

Four.

"Just stop for a second."

Matt put his hand on my elbow, and I placed my foot on the next step.

The moment slowed. My vision narrowed. The anger was a pinpoint.

I moved before I even knew what I was doing. I twisted around to face him, holding the water glass steady in my left hand.

Whack! The back of my right hand collided with his right cheek. *Smack!* My palm firmly slapped his left cheek in the quickest one-two punch neither of us could have predicted. "I will never wait up for you again." My finger jabbed the air in front of his nose.

Surprise, almost delight, played in his eyes. *Ah, what newfound fun do we have here? She thinks she wants to dance?* Matt tilted back and stumbled down one step.

I turned and continued to climb the stairs. The water in the glass had sloshed. It hadn't spilled. I was surprised I was barely shaking. I smiled as my feet found the next step. *What?! Did I just smack him in the face?* It felt good, scary good. This was the first race of justice in my veins I had felt in years. I felt a glimpse of my power and will, this strength I have.

It scared me that I slapped him. It scared me because I enjoyed it. *Jeez, this can't be healthy.*

Then fear clouded in. *Fuck. What have I done?* I marched up the stairs, not showing any hesitation. *What is he going to do? Maybe that was a mistake. Will we be brawling again? Is he going to attack me from behind? While I sleep?*

I didn't look back. I had made my statement with landed blows. I walked surely to the bedroom and drank the water down. I tucked myself in, laid as close to the edge as possible, pulled the pillow into a bundled pile, and shoved it under my head. *Fuck that motherfucker.*

My heart was racing. All my senses were on high alert. I heard Dan mumble something to Matt and the front door open and close. The car started up, and they were gone.

I closed and opened my eyes. Blinking back my disbelief.

He's gone.

I slapped my husband and lived.

I looked around the room. Everything looked the same, yet it was all different. Matt had been physical with me many times before, and I was thankful he had a friend over, as it might've ended differently. I may not have survived.

The presence of another person probably saved me from dying in my sleep. I knew this. Things were going to change; the power was shifting. I fell into a deep restful sleep.

CLAW BACK

Little steps helped me gain ground. The first realization came in the quiet car with the dead radio. I admitted to myself I was being abused. Ashlei was being abused.

The verbal abuse was constant. Physical abuse was not as often, but the threat was always there. Shoving and pushing occurred, which somehow I did not define as physical abuse. I mean, he did not hit me with an open or fisted hand. An imaginary boundary of physical abuse comes with "hitting." Even now I have a hard time saying I was physically abused. Shoving me and lifting me against a wall were physical, and they happened often enough. The near-death choking was physical. The bellowing man and constant belittling caused damage too, maybe more. Much like an AA attendee, I had to first admit it. I was abused. I also had to extrapolate the truth to include Ashlei. Olivia was too young to be included in the behaviors, but I had allowed Ashlei to be verbally abused. I owned that. I did put a stop to it, but it had gone on long enough for other people to notice it and be worried. A thick paste of guilt sat atop my conscience.

My focus was now on my girls. I had to claw back myself, my strength, my confidence so I could take care of my children. I went about my business, actively ignoring him to the best of my ability. I logged the events in the ledger of my mind and felt stronger.

Each step. Small steps. Little steps carry us forward. With each dig from Matt, I told myself the truth. *No, Matt, I am not stupid; in fact, I am quite intelligent and have loads of common sense. No, Matt, I am not a slob; in fact, I cleaned the kitchen and did all of the dishes. I have a great job and bring home a decent paycheck. I pay for and take care of everything here.*

Each small step gained me ground. Grew my fortitude and self-reliance. It was not only helpful, but foundational, that at work I was a rock star. I was loved and supported by friends and family too. It was Matt whom I had let define my worth, my value. Abuse is like that. The psychology of abuse changes the neural pathways in your brain. You start to believe you deserve to be treated this way. You believe somehow you brought on the anger. And if you could only do everything right, there would be no yelling, no harm. If I could clean well enough, be quieter, be a better cook, be thin enough, and show more common sense, then everything would be fine. My list of required improvements was long. I had to be a better communicator. I had to be less forgetful, cleaner, prettier, funnier, and sexier. I put the blame on myself, but this was a lie—a lie I believed.

I am, you are, we are beautiful, amazing, and powerful beings and deserve to be treated with love and respect. I state it again, for myself and you, my treasured reader.

We are beautiful, amazing, and powerful beings and deserve to be treated with love and respect.

It is the truth. I can say it now, years after being with Matt. I deserve to be treated with love and respect. I deserve to be treated with love and respect. You do too. You deserve love and respect. We all do.

The way back was with baby steps. I washed the dishes the way I wanted. I arranged the fridge and cabinets the way I wanted. I did not turn all of the cans to face the same direction. I made the dinners I wanted to make. I was becoming me. I clawed myself back with tiny steps, day by day.

I sought out help and support. I talked to a friend at work, and I spoke with our pastor. I told our pastor about Matt's infidelity. He informed me I had an "out." If a spouse had an affair, the other spouse could seek a divorce without losing favor with God. I am not sure this is typical Christian doctrine. Did I tell the pastor about the abuse? No. I was barely admitting it to myself. I did not tell anyone about it. I did not tell my mom. I did not tell my friends. It was embarrassing. I did not tell anyone about the physical stuff that happened at our house. Matt's parents knew because they were the ones who often got called to come defuse the situation or pick up the girls. The pastor gave me one piece of advice: "Do whatever it takes to be able to look your daughters in the eye and say you did everything you could to make it work." Maybe had I told him about the abuse, he would have given me different advice. I doubt it.

I took the message to heart and committed myself and my effort to doing whatever it took before hitting the divorce button, even after I felt I had made the decision when he left the Indy 500 messages. Matt and I talked. I'm not sure how serious Matt was, but we did make some progress. Matt started taking Prozac, and he tried to slow his drug use. We saw a counselor for a few months. These activities were temporary, such were our cycles of relationship.

These cycles partially explain why I stayed so long. He would get better, it would be okay, he would be sort of sober, and I was an optimist. I always assumed things would improve. He would plan and convince me it was an upward swing. Then two or three months in, we would slide sideways, and the same bad behaviors and habits reappeared. The counseling, Prozac, and his sobriety fell away, and we were back at it. The same patterns. Drugs, wrath, and infidelity were our lives. The small acts of standing up for myself were received as defiance. When Matt's irritation at me did not receive the appropriate response or contriteness, his anger grew.

The summer burned hot and heavy. I was accomplished at work, and Matt was slipping further into his own mire. By the fall, things were worse. Violence raged. Drunken late nights were common. Matt's parents came and rescued me and the girls with growing frequency. I was too embarrassed to ask Mom or my friends for help. I was ashamed I had not done something sooner. *Why was I tolerating this? Why was I allowing myself and my children to be exposed to this?*

A Saturday night in late September, we were fighting again. Matt was drunk, and the girls were crying. Olivia was just over a year old, Ashlei nearly eight. They had been hiding in Ashlei's room, with Ashlei protecting her little sister from the screaming downstairs. The wind whipped the dark windows, and a storm was brewing outside. Inside it was already blowing.

Crash.

Matt pushed me in the kitchen. I stumbled into the table, and plates broke on the floor. The corner of the table pierced my hipbone. I held my hip, lost my balance, and fell to my knees. He kicked the kitchen table and then the chair, knocking it over. I crawled into the living room. He stepped over me and slid his hand across the desk and whooshed everything on it onto the floor. With papers fluttering down around me, I scramble-crab-walked backwards until my shoulder bumped into the coffee table, skewing the perfect angle at which it had been placed.

"Matt . . ." My left hand on the table, I rose. I extended my right hand as a barrier to his advancing form. "It's okay . . ."

Push. My shoulders shoved backwards. He pushed me again. I did not fall this time. I was cornered at the bottom of the stairs.

"Stop! Stop!" Ashlei screamed from midway down the stairs. "Stop it, Daddy! Stop it!" She held Olivia in her arms. "You have to stop it, Daddy!" She sobbed and panted, shaking, holding on tight to her wailing baby sister.

"Get upstairs, Ashlei! This is none of your business," he boomed.

Instead she ran down to me. I clutched her and Olivia to my legs. I faced Matt while lifting Olivia out of Ashlei's arms.

"What do you think you're doing?" Matt strode towards us. "You think these kids will protect you?"

"Stop, Daddy! Stop!"

I wrapped my arm around Olivia, holding her tight to me, her face buried in my left boob. Ashlei clung to my right side, gripping my waist. My right arm slung around her, with my fingers in her armpit, pulling her to me. Me. My girls. *These are my girls, and you will not hurt them.*

Matt lunged for me. Gripped his hands around my

throat. His fingers clamped down. Teeth gritted. Screaming, spitting. Rage purpled his face. Squeezing. My hyoid bone pushing back into my windpipe. I did not fight back. I held on tight. I did not loosen the hold on my girls. Both of them howling now. I blinked back tears, clenched my jaw and stared at him. *You will have to kill me while looking at me.*

His eyes were unseeing. Adrenaline sheen. Shiny, dilated pupils. Not there.

Squeeze. Constrict.

Spots. Tunnel. Gasp.

If he does not stop soon, I will pass out and drop Olivia.

Ashlei let go with her right hand and flailed at him, still grasping my waist with her left arm. She gave a small kick in his direction. She shouted, "Let go, Daddy, let go!"

She closed her hand back around me, and I regripped my hold onto her.

My babies. My babies are going to see me die.

This time it was not calmness I felt; it was sadness. Whole racking sadness and fear. A black pit yawning to swallow me.

They are seeing me die right now.

I will die and not get to raise my girls.

I have to be with my girls. My babies. He has to stop.

I did not let go of them. I seized them tighter. I did not fight him even as my vision narrowed. I stood there taking the strangling. Holding my girls.

My girls are seeing their mom die. No.

Blackness closing in. There was no air. Another little kick from Ashlei.

"Stop, Daddy! Stop! You are hurting her!" she wailed. "STOP!"

He broke eye contact. Looked at Ashlei. He threw me backward, letting go of my neck. He shook his head to loosen the fury. See the moment. His presence returned.

I fell backward and sat hard on the bottom stair. Olivia in my lap and Ashlei crumpled next to me.

Matt darted out of the door into the garage.

Gasping. Coughing. Choking. Eyes watering with the newfound air.

I did not let go of Olivia. Ashlei disentangled from me and scrambled for the phone.

She called 911. Then called her grandparents.

Within minutes everyone was there trying to figure out what had happened. Matt was pacing the garage. He had not fled. I told the police I did not want to press charges. "No one wants that," his mom whispered. The house emptied. The police left.

I found myself in the garage with Mike, Matt's dad. "You know, you don't have to do this," Mike said quietly. "You don't have to live this way."

Tears dried to my face. Shock taking over. My mind blank. I said nothing.

"You deserve better. The girls deserve better. We love you and are proud of you."

The tears started again. *What was wrong with me?* I had already decided. I knew I had to make the break. But I hadn't yet gotten us away.

My heart ached. My heart ached for the moment. For what my daughters saw, what I allowed them to see. Why hadn't I left sooner? It could not happen again. I had to survive. I had to live. I had to raise these girls. They were my responsibility. I cannot die at the hands of their father in front of them.

Monday morning, I called in sick to work and went to an attorney. "I need to file for divorce."

Flash Forward:
Goal Setting

"Let's get serious now," I instruct.

"Mom, really?"

"Yes, we are going to do this." I open the wooden book and flip to the next blank pages. "We do this every year. I don't know why you are acting so surprised."

Olivia groans and settles into the large sofa. Lauren snuggles onto Olivia's lap. Lauren is too young to participate. We will talk about her goals for the year anyway.

"Got the coffee." Ashlei sets my cup down on the coffee table and scoots in next to Olivia.

Brad is seated on the small couch, bouncing his leg, waiting to get started. "Come here, Brooke." He waves her over, and she climbs into his lap. At least that stops his leg from bouncing.

"Okay! We'll look at our goals from last year, then talk about this coming year," I start off. "Do we want to review the family goals first?"

"That's a great place to start," Brad replies, as Ashlei agrees and Olivia shrugs. The two littler ones look at their big sisters and smile.

Ashlei takes a sip of her coffee and leans in.

We do this annually. Each year we discuss what our goals are for us as a family and as individuals. Brad and I outline our goals as a couple too. I've been doing this course of action for years. At work, it's common to do annual goal setting and mid-cycle reviews. How many people do it at home with their families, I have no idea.

With my tumultuous background, it surprises some people that goal setting is a skill long since trained in me by my mom. My mother was many things, for sure, and my upbringing was anything but normal. Mom always believed in me, encouraged me, and taught me to set goals and desires for myself. I believe this has been a key component to success and the ability to escape certain aspects of my life.

I have been doing goal setting for as long as I can remember. When I was a single mom, I started doing this process with Ashlei and Olivia as well. Olivia was two years old when we first started, so hers were written for her. Ashlei has had clear goals for herself since she was eight or nine.

The first time I did this sit-down with Brad, he was a bit skeptical. He says he tried to take it seriously, but thought it felt forced. We were not even married yet. The New Year was early in our dating cycle, which is the typical time to think about goal setting. After his initial hesitation, he now enthusiastically engages and looks forward to the process for himself, us as a couple, and the family. Brad and I have continued to do this with our four children and, although there is some good-natured grousing, I hope they enjoy it and know it's meaningful.

Brad is eager to summarize accomplishments and shares with our girls the satisfaction of clarity that goal setting provides. Clear targets, measurable and true. Recently Brad read an article he keeps quoting to us, "You are 40 percent more likely to achieve your goals if you write them down."

Since Brad and I have been together, we have a special family goal book that we pull out each year. Now our youngest, Lauren, seeks out the goal book and looks forward to the review and goal-setting activity.

This exercise is not the answer to all life's complications and hardships. It does provide directional targets and guideposts for who we want to be. The practice urges me, and us, to reflect, to be conscious about our choices. And goal setting helps prioritize time throughout the year.

"All right, family," I begin. "We said we were going to eat dinner together at least four out of seven nights a week. How did we do this year?"

Goals do not have to be life changing. They can be boundaries. They can be aspirational. Our goals range from the mundane, as in eating dinner as a family, to the big dreams of writing and launching a book. Or getting promotions, starting new jobs, getting all A's, or saving X number of dollars. Specific goals are needed to provide the clarity and focus. "Soft goals" are harder to measure, however, yet they can be directional and useful. "Be nicer to your sister" is a common goal for our children. Stating that objective helps set expectations and a foundation of kindness.

I don't know how my life might have turned out without goal setting. I'm glad we do it. I'm grateful Brad joins me in leading our family with clarity and love. My hope for my girls is they will keep this tradition and it will serve them as well as it has served me.

"All right, now what's next? Let's see—how many family vacations do we want to take this year?"

SELL THE BED

The marriage was not over that day. Not the day of the messages. Not the day I slapped Matt. Not the day of the choking. Not the day of going to the attorney. It was not over for months. Years.

I had all of the power; I just did not know it. The condo was in my name. I had a great job and made good money. My power at home had been diminished, though, lost in the fear of violence, maybe even death. Matt did not lay a hand on the girls. But they did see and hear too much.

I had started divorce proceedings. But I went the soft route. Matt had no idea I had seen an attorney. The final draft of divorce papers was ready in October. I did not tell him. I started a negotiation in my mind to get him out. Gently. Passively. So no one got hurt, namely me.

We had agreed we needed time apart and that he would move out by the first of November. He was clueless that I had the divorce papers ready. I started buying items for him to take to a new place, a set of dishes, kitchen utensils, dish towels, and bath towels. I stacked the stuff in the garage.

He did not move out.

We set a new date, the first of December. I bought a couch. A silverware set. I bought a small set of pans, although he never cooked. The garage pile grew. I was nice. So nice. Too nice.

December first came and went. He did not leave.

We agreed to wait until after the holidays. The day after Christmas included another explosion. He was not around on New Year's, but had not moved out.

The temporary new Matt made an appearance. He said he loved me. He loved the girls. He wanted to be a family. He told this to Ashlei. He told this to his mom. I was the bad guy for making him leave, for upending our family.

His actions did not support his words. He stayed out most nights. Came home drunk and coked up. His escapades grew in frequency and debauchery. He was to move out on February first. I bought coffee cups. I bought bathroom rugs. I bought some toilet paper. The garage was filling.

The February date came and went. Matt was still there.

I played along. We laughed and joked. It was amicable. I was passive. When we talked about him moving out, it was easy, no fighting. It was an agreement. Yes, we were going to do this. We knew it was right. He was going to move out on March first.

He did not go.

Why is he still here? What am I going to do? How am I going to get him out of here? He said he would move out on April first. I found him an apartment. I told him I would pay for the first month's rent and deposit. He did not go.

The garage was loaded with everything he needed.

He did not leave.

I never thought to ask the attorney what to do. I had the divorce papers ready. They had been ready for months.

May first and Matt was still not gone. I was willing to pay for an apartment for him. He had a garage full of goods for his new place. I had to get creative. What does it take to get him out without getting him mad? Without a big fight? Without police presence?

I pushed the subject of him leaving and made it clear by no longer having sex with him. I think that was the first time he realized I was serious. Or the first time he admitted it to himself. No more sex meant something to him. Once he knew I was serious, he turned it around. He threatened to take the girls from me, of which I was terrified. His parents were rich, or at least I thought they were. He intimidated me with their wealth and power. He declared I wouldn't see the girls ever again. I was convinced Matt would at least try, and it would be a drawn-out custody battle. Even though this was illogical, I was still full of fear that this could happen. Maybe he would try to take them out of spite, even if he did not want to do the work it took to care for them. They would end up living with his mom.

I was small, but I was growing. I was taking myself back. I was taking my girls back. And it took years to see through the psychosis I was in. I believed his lie that he could take away my daughters. But I believed in myself a tiny bit more, and it was enough. Enough to know I could not live with him, and my children deserved better. I knew it was best for us if he left.

As a last-ditch effort of passive action, I sold our bedroom furniture. I slept with Ashlei in her double bed. Matt slept on the couch for three nights.

He moved out.

I should have thought of it sooner. When all else fails, sell the bed.

ICE CREAM CAR RIDES

Life was immediately better, happier, easier. Ashlei, Olivia, and I could breathe, play, and not fear getting screamed at. There were no late-night drunken fights. We were not tiptoeing around Matt's moods.

Since it was turning into summer, we got ice cream at the Dairy Queen almost every night. We drove around in our Toyota Camry looking at houses we wanted to live in. We got twist cones, and Olivia sat in the middle-back, her ice cream in a cup. Sometimes if it was a weekend, we went to the Chocolate Moose and got ice cream with eyes.

Matt did not come around much. He did not see his girls on "his weekends." It was more fluid than a scheduled plan. He came by occasionally, for an hour or two, then would yell at me at the front door until he was tired, then leave. I was definitely the bad guy. I had made him move out. He and his mom convinced Ashlei that I should have let him stay, and told her I was a homewrecker. It was my job as the wife to hold it all together, regardless of what was happening.

I didn't serve him the divorce papers immediately. Matt did not seem to understand, or acknowledge, what was going on. He had moved out, which was good. He was not paying any child support, which was expected. He was up and down. Friendly, then furious. Happy, then fuming. He came by early one Sunday morning, reeking of alcohol and the stink of a bar, but in a good mood.

"Hey, Hopey! Ashlei and Olivia here?"

"No, Ashlei is not here. Olivia is." Of course, I thought, she is a baby. It's Sunday morning, where would she be if she was not with me?

He pushed his way inside and scooped up Olivia. He tickled and giggled and kissed on her with his smelly mouth. She did not mind, nor know any better. He was her dad.

"I have a friend in the car. I want Olivia to meet her."

"Who is it?"

"I met her last night. Hope, you'll love her. She is so much fun!" He headed to the door.

"Wait." I was gentle, not reproving, sweet. "Do you think she is going to be your girlfriend for a while?"

"Huh? I don't know. Shit. Who knows?" He shrugged at me.

"Okay, well, let's not introduce her to Olivia today. Does this gal work at Night Moves?"

"Yeah," Matt looked surprised. "How did you know? Do you know her?"

"No, Matt, I'm just guessing. It's almost seven in the morning, obviously you've been out all night, you stink, and you brought a girl here. I can connect the dots." I was not angry. I was resigned. This was easy conversation, no yelling, no fighting.

"All right. All right." Matt nuzzled and kissed Olivia one more time, set her down, and she toddled to me. "I want to see the girls this week."

"We'll set it up," I smiled, knowing he wouldn't come through, and shut the door behind him. I looked at Olivia hugging my legs. I lifted her to my hip and carried her upstairs. "Let's get you cleaned up, sugar plum." I had to get the smoky scent off of her. I was too lenient with Matt, too patient. Still an enabler, but at least this exchange ended the way I wanted. Olivia did not have to meet the topless dancer in his car, and Matt did not get mad and throw a fit.

A few weeks later, I had the divorce papers served. That exchange was not so smooth.

A sheriff served him the papers at his jobsite. How they knew where this was is beyond me; too bad they could not find him later when he was delinquent on his child support. Matt stormed into the house demanding to know why I wanted a divorce. It was insane. Did he really think we were getting back together? Yes! He thought we were on a break, that we were just separated. He said he did not want a divorce. I reminded him he brought a dancer (or a prostitute) to the house a few weeks prior. How did bringing her signal a desire to get back together?

After a loud back and forth, I convinced him to hold onto the papers and to have an attorney look at them, and we could talk about it again in a few weeks.

Gently, easily, softly, I followed up each week or so. Had he reviewed them? When was he going to sign them? Had he had an attorney look at them? The answer was always no. The papers were drafted in October, and it wasn't until July when I had them served. It was now becoming fall, and the papers were still not signed.

I went over to his apartment to pick up Olivia's blanket, left there on a rare visit, and brought the papers with me. I needed him to sign them. I wanted it to be legally done. I needed it to be over.

Matt was still resistant. He said he did not want to be divorced. I told him it would take months for the judge to approve anyway. I urged him to sign and I would mail them in.

"It will take forever before they are finalized."

"I will sign them if you have sex with me," Matt said, not joking.

"C'mon, Matt. Just sign. It will be months before it's final."

"No, I'm serious. Have sex with me right here, right now, and I will sign the papers."

I glanced around at the no one who was there. The sparse apartment. Considering options.

What could it hurt? We had been together eleven years. One last go wouldn't change my life. I was staying celibate and not going on dates for at least a year anyway. The last thing I wanted was another man to deal with.

"Sure," I deadpanned.

"All right then. Give me the papers."

We fucked on the couch.

I flipped to the page with the line for his signature, and he signed the papers. I submitted them the next day, which was a Friday. The judge signed it on Monday, and a week later we got the finalized decree.

Matt was pissed. He called me a liar because I had told him it would take months. He called me some other choice words. It didn't matter because it was done. The divorce was final. The girls and I were free. Not yet safe. Not yet out of the woods, but we were legally unbound.

Ashlei was getting a steady diet of lies from Matt and his mom about why we got divorced. Yes, she had witnessed the fighting and the violence. She herself had called the police and his parents more than once. But a child wants their parents together, and her dad and grandmother were telling her that was best.

I read every book I got my hands on about children of divorce. How to support them, how to raise them. I read books specific for each child's age. I wanted to take care of Ashlei and not let further damage happen. Matt was an inconsistent presence in their lives. All of the guidance I consumed said it was best for the kids to have a relationship with both parents. The Children of Divorce class I had to take said the same. Ashlei was seeing two therapists, one at school and one outside of school. And still it was a struggle.

She fought me to escape the house. Matt's mom lived close enough she could run there if she got out the door. Each time Matt dropped her off, Ashlei had a crying fit, punctuated with Matt's rage and proclamation that I broke the family. Then Ashlei hid in her room until I could coax her out with food or TV. It was hard, so these quiet times in the car were good. We spent time driving around, eating ice cream, looking for our next home and dreaming.

Work was a saving grace. A mentor let me know I had natural skills, and I should go into leadership. I was excelling at Lilly. I launched a new microbiology laboratory. I was in the throes of career development learning. The hard part was driving back and forth to Indy. The sixty-minute commute, which had saved me and gotten me to this point, made for a long day. The girls were commonly the first to be dropped off at daycare and the last to be picked up. Since I had the girls full time, it made for a full day, a full life, for all of us girls.

If something needed to be done for the house, I did it. I replaced a washer and put two new faucets in. Determined to do it all on my own, I paid my bills, fed my kids, fixed my car, and managed my home. I was fine. The girls were good. We did not need a man, we did not need anyone for anything. I plowed forward with determination and focus. I could do this. The hours were long and exhausting, but we were making it.

Then Daniel, a previous boss, reached out to me. "Hope! Come work for me again. I can pay you now!" Baxter had bought the Cook pharmaceutical manufacturing plant in Bloomington that I had worked at previously. This was perfect because it was fifteen minutes from my home and the job came with better pay. I left Eli Lilly. I owe so much to my experience there. I developed a deep expertise in pharmaceutical microbiology and environmental monitoring, started learning the art of managing up, massive cross functional interaction, and launched my career development and growth there. Although it was a tough decision, it was the right thing for the girls and me. Being a single parent, working closer to home and their school was important. I started back as a Microbiology Analyst II at Baxter with a small raise. If there was a school event, I could make it without having to take a day off. And this position had the added benefit of working for Daniel, who is one of the best bosses I have ever had and one of the greatest people I know.

Soon after, I was promoted to supervise one microbiology laboratory. The position grew, and I became a manager of the lab. Then I managed three microbiology laboratories. Each job change came with an increase in responsibility, title, and pay. We were driving improvements. We reduced cycle times, reduced error rates, and increased productivity. It was a blast. The success at work continued to fuel my confidence and growth at home. I had proven to myself I could do it. I got stronger. I stopped loaning money to Matt. I stopped making excuses for him. I finally realized he had no power, nor desire, to take the girls from me. He could barely take care of himself. His life deteriorated quickly. There were stints in jail. Car crashes and repossessions. Drunk driving and abandoning the scene of a crime in a borrowed car.

The girls were growing, blossoming, excelling. We had kept up our ice cream drives, and one night we saw a house for sale by owner in a neighborhood we liked. I made an appointment the next day and made an offer on the spot. I kept ownership of the condo and rented it out to two young men I knew from work. I now had two homes. The car was paid for. I had two beautiful daughters, and I was on my way. My life was amazing. I was free from Matt.

Were we really free?

MERMAID WITH WINGS

The blue house, small and cozy, was ours. We each had our own bedroom, and mine had a tiny master bath. The three of us together, we could do anything. It was us against the world. I left the house around 7:00 a.m. each day. Ashlei was responsible for getting herself and Olivia onto the school bus. I dutifully left work by five o'clock each night, so they were not left unattended for too long.

Our new home, eighteen hundred square feet, with a fenced-in backyard and a play set, was in the well-known, populated neighborhood of Sherwood Oaks. Growing up, I thought it was where rich people lived. I was making decent money and lived within my means, so I guess you could say we were rich. I was queen of my castle, with my princesses to help.

We did it all ourselves. We painted the two bathrooms with vivid colors—my inner hippie comes out when I paint. We did up Olivia's room in a pale pink, complete with castles and fairies. Any maintenance needed for the house

I did or hired in. I didn't accept help from Matt, not that he would come through on his promises anyway. He liked to talk a big game in front of the girls, show them he was willing to help. I did not need him. My girls and I could take care of ourselves.

Each spring, I backed Mom's truck up to the house, climbed onto the roof, and cleaned out the gutters. I took the same truck and got mulch at the dirt racetrack on the south side of town. I shoveled the stinking stuff from the truck bed onto a tarp that I drug around the yard to mulch the flower beds. Sweaty, dirty, heavy work. I reveled in it. The first two years in the blue house we tried a garden. The soil was clay, and unlike Mom with her dirt growing skills, we gave up the garden efforts. I paid a neighborhood kid twenty bucks to mow the lawn. The yard was not showcase beautiful, but fine for us. One year we got an unprecedented snowfall (eighteen inches!), and I had no snow shovel. I attempted to clear the snow with the edge of a Swiffer. Two dads from nearby came and shoveled the drive. The next morning there was a snow shovel left outside my garage. The neighbors came in handy the day the on-demand-water-heater inlet broke and I was at work. The girls were home after school. Water poured into our laundry room, into the living room, and seeped into the kitchen. The girls did their best with the same Swiffer, every towel in the house, and finally resorted to Pizza Express cups to scoop out the water.

Ashlei ran to the neighbor's house, and the guy two doors down came and shut off the water. From then on, each of us always knows where the water main is in our houses.

The house and neighborhood were perfect. Halloween proved lively both for trick-or-treating and for working the door (which is my favorite part). Kids the girls' ages lived nearby so there was always someone for them to play with. Our immediate next-door neighbor had three kids, and one was Olivia's age, Annie. They became best friends. The girls traipsed unfettered between the homes, in and out of the backyard and sliding back doors. We took walks around the one-mile loop of the neighborhood. I gave them brown paper sacks to collect treasures on our walks. Usually pine-cones were collected, and occasionally they discovered a bird nest or something more exotic.

One afternoon I was taking our loop walk with the two six-year-olds. Annie and Olivia had their trusty brown bags, and they found a robin's egg. They both wanted to put the egg in their bag. Olivia was easy to share, and she let Annie take it. Olivia was magical and had a huge imagination, while Annie was literal and practical.

"I want to be a bird when I grow up," Olivia said in an awed voice.

"You cannot be a bird," Annie declared. "You are a human. You cannot be a bird."

A small sigh emitted from Olivia. We kept walking, and I kept eavesdropping.

Olivia took her time. "Okay, if I can't be a bird, I want to be a mermaid!"

I heard the satisfaction in her voice.

"Ha! Mermaids don't even exist! You cannot be a mermaid."

"Well, then I want to be a mermaid with wings!" Olivia announced, triumphant.

I could almost hear Annie roll her eyes. She did not respond and kept walking. Olivia was a dreamer. And practical Annie could not squelch her. We did have to have a serious talk with Annie and her parents when Annie told Olivia that Santa did not exist. Santa was real at our house, and I could not have the practicality of Olivia's best friend burst her bubble. Annie explained to me that Santa was not real, just like Jesus was not real—which was interesting because I knew it would freak out her uber-conservative Christian parents that she believed Jesus was as fake as Santa. I chose not to take on the Jesus discussion but handled the Santa issue with her parents. Olivia believed in Santa until she was thirteen (Ashlei did until age ten), and that was a win in my estimation.

My life centered around the girls. Everything I did, I did with them or for them. Work was a large component, of course, because I was the sole breadwinner. Each day was work, school, homework, dinner, cheer practice, board games, card games, and playing with the neighbors. We did our chores on Saturday mornings. I cleaned the kitchen, living room, and my room. The girls had to clean their rooms and the two bathrooms. We had one other small room in the house, what might be called a den, and we kept it empty for throw pillows and gymnastics.

Often it happens that, as in our case, single moms and their eldest child work together to run the house. Ashlei started dinner most evenings. Our meals were not complicated. We made chicken and vegetables most nights. Usually with noodles too. Garlic salt and Italian seasoning. Ashlei helped take care of Olivia. We called her baby, until she was seven. "Do you have the baby?" "Yes, Mom, I have the baby." Most nights we all fell asleep in Olivia's daybed with the fairies watching over us. We read three books each night, and I would fight to stay awake; by the end of the books, we would all be asleep in the tiny bed. At some point I got into my own bed, with Ashlei soon following.

Both girls were on cheer squads. Tuesday, Thursday, and Saturday had us racing out to the gym to drop them off for practice. Although they later have said we were always late, I remember mostly being on time. The cheer season also had us traveling the Midwest, spending weekends in other cities during the competition season. And once a year we went to Florida with the team for a competition at Disney

World. This event was good on many levels, and it forced me to get it together to take the kids on a vacation. The first year we went, I could afford only three nights, with horrible early and late-night flights. The second year, I could swing four nights. And so it went. The final year we were there, we stayed ten nights and drove to the coast for the back half of the trip.

This way of life might have been how Mom felt the one year she was single. It was us against the world, and her world centered around us. Mom had sat on the miniature red couch in a little house and set up her typewriter to make a living. My job was a full-blown career and was starting to blossom, and my daughters knew the importance of my work. I don't think they knew about me finding the confidence at work that led to building strength at home, ultimately empowering me to divorce Matt. All the same, the girls knew my job was important and they respected my accomplishments.

My employment was practically important too. Matt did not pay child support. My parents, nor his parents, gave us any money. No one was helping financially. If something had to get done, I had to pay for it. I lived within my means, exactly within my means. Cheer was expensive. I did not have an expensive car or do outlandish things. I did not have credit cards. The house and student loans were the only debt I carried. I figured I would have to pay the student loan until I died.

I did not have a goal of a specific dollar amount I wanted to make. Men, it seems, commonly set their goals with pay targets. They seem to want to make X dollars by X age. My goals were career driven based on responsibility and impact. Goals for pay and title came later after a certain measure of success had been achieved.

Baxter paid me well, and I continued to get promoted. I moved through the ranks of leadership from supervisor, to manager, then managing multiple laboratories. My drive for order, creative problem-solving, and improved performance put me on the "show-and-tell" tour. Whenever corporate visitors or clients came through the facility, they made a stop at our microbiology labs. We talked about the tests we performed, our low error rates, quick turnaround times, and increased productivity. With this skill in hand, my boss, Bill, asked me to do continuous improvement for the whole site as a "trial run." I set up a support structure for the three lab supervisors to keep everything running and took on the temporary assignment.

This is an important lesson I share now with people I mentor. If an opportunity arrives at your door, by a leader in the organization, it should be seriously considered for several reasons. Number one, if the leader approaches you, they have seen the skill and capability within you to execute their vision. Number two, the leader is with you on this journey; by moving you into the trial role, they are putting their support behind you and will not let you fail. Number three, HOLY MOLY, it is fun to go and do new and exciting things. New challenges, new people to meet, and new problems to fix. And the best growth happens when you are outside of your comfort zone.

I was in the temporary role for about three months when I approached Bill and told him he should either give me the job or move me back to run the labs. I could not do both effectively. He gave me the job, the title, and a pay raise to boot. I was driving continuous improvement for the 1000-person site. We had 9 filling lines, building 4 more, and we were a 24/5 operation. It was exciting, and I was thrilled for the new challenge.

As my career progressed, I learned how to dress professionally, how to do my hair so it was not so untamed, and how to partner closer and better with colleagues. I was still deploying the methods of establishing relationship accounts, taught to me by my first boss. I made deposits into relationship accounts before I made withdrawals. I invested in people. I made every attempt to partner shamelessly and closely with everyone. I gave my team credit for wins and took responsibility for failures. You cannot succeed at work without help, and the same is true at home. There are many people helping you along the way. Friendly neighbors who turn off the water main, wonderful colleagues who confide you are too bossy, and family who help love and care for your kids.

This period was a time of substantial growth in courage, faith, hope, and joy. Being on my own after the damage of abuse was powerful. I developed so much during this period. I was focused on being successful, showing the world I could raise my girls, being a professional working woman, and forgoing a man in our life.

I was not going to ever make myself small again. I was never going to let my children be belittled and see pain in their home. Several years after the divorce, Matt made himself a New Year's Resolution that he would take the girls every other weekend. And he did.

The first weekend I was alone, I had no idea what to do. I cleaned the house obsessively and worried if the girls were okay. After several weekends, I cleaned on the first day they were gone and then relaxed on the couch and read the newspaper. Who could imagine relaxing and reading the newspaper on the couch on a Saturday morning?! I began to look forward to the weekends without the kids. I was becoming a person, not just a mom. I went to the store without someone with me. I exercised on my own schedule, watched whatever I wanted, and ate whenever I wanted. It was wonderful. I had a group of girlfriends, and we enjoyed hanging out together. We camped, we did spa days, we went mudding one year. We jumped out of an airplane together. It was incredible and created a bond of friendship with those lovely ladies that runs true today.

My trust in myself at work grew, and I continued to transfer that to my homelife. Those weekends alone were the first time I was ever living alone, ever, even for just two days. Maybe it was an extrapolation of the two hours in the quiet car; the alone time gave me myself.

For a solid two years, Matt took them on his weekends. But then he lost hold of his resolution and slipped back into inconsistency. For two years, though, my daughters got to know their dad.

OLIVIA'S STORY

Glancing up from my phone, I look at the rundown house Dad disappeared into fifteen minutes ago. He said it would be five minutes. What's he doing in there? I return to scrolling the Gram, flicking through vines. We're going to be late to the movie.

I have to pee.

I look up again at the house in this sketchy neighborhood. I don't know where we are. This is no longer my hometown, and I have not been to this area before anyway, I don't think. Dad told me to sit in the car and wait. I've got to go. Literally.

I don't see any movement inside the house. No people, no noise, nothing. This little house looks plain and sad and neglected. The screen door is hanging off the hinges and looks like it could fall off any second.

I really have to pee.

Twenty-five minutes he's been in there. Five more minutes, and I'm going to get out and go up there. *What can he be doing?*

I switch to Snapchat and catch up with a few friends.

Five minutes pass, still no Dad, and I'm squirming in

the seat. *I'm gonna see what is taking so long and find the bathroom.*

I climb out of the car and go through the open chain link gate, thankful there is no dog. The fence is wrecked anyway, nothing that could hold an animal in. I walk to the broken screen door, curious and timid. And confused.

The real door behind the screen door is dirty and open a little bit. I don't hear anything. I knock on the doorframe to make my presence known.

"Hello? Hey, Dad! It's me. Let's go!"

No answer. I gently open the door to peek in. "Dad? Anybody? Hello?"

The living room is gloomy, and I see the shape of a couch on the far wall. *Is that a person lying on the couch?*

"Hello? Dad?" I say louder. "Hey! Anyone home?"

No answer. No movement from the couch. I stand in the doorway. It looks like it could be Dad on the couch. I don't see anyone else.

"Dad!" I am near yelling. "Hello! Anybody? Hello!"

Dad falls asleep easily, and it's not strange to see him resting on a couch. But now? We are supposed to go to a movie. What's he doing here? What is this house? Where is this neighborhood? Why I am waiting in the car? What is going on?

My gut feels sick. Worry washes over me. Something is wrong. No one is answering. "DAD!" I yell one more time.

I walk over the matted, stained carpet to the couch. Dad. He's passed out.

"Dad, wake up." *What is going on?* I bend to shake him awake. "Dad?" I push his shoulders. He feels cold. The left side of his face looks blue.

"Dad!" I shriek. "Dad! Wake up! Dad!" I place my hands on his chest, and I lean my ear to his mouth.

No breath. No heartbeat.

Tears stream down my face. I scream again. "Is anybody here?! Help!"

I shake him, harder than I wanted to. No response. Nothing.

"Dad! Wake up!"

I pull him to the floor. Harder than I wanted to.

"Help!" I scream again.

I start chest compressions. My CPR certification renewal in freshman health class, three weeks ago, has me on autopilot.

"Dad! You have to wake up."

1-2-3-4.

I push his chin back, pinch his nose, and place my mouth over his. I push two breaths.

5-6-7-8.

"Help me!" I scream to no one.

Two women and a toddler appear from a back bedroom.

"What happened?" I shriek. "Call 911!"

I am in a dream. There is only here. Only now.

"Dad! You have to wake up!"

Pinch nose. I force two breaths into him.

"Call 911!" I screech again.

1-2-3-4.

"What happened to him?"

"He was fine. He was just going to lay down for a minute," one of the women utters. "Who are you?"

"I'M HIS DAUGHTER!"

"Dad! You have to wake up . . ."

5-6-7-8.

Tears blur my vision. Fear bubbles up my throat and threatens to seize me.

"Dad! You have to wake up . . ."

Pinch nose. Two breaths.

My arms feel like noodles. I am weak. Panicked. Fear blossoming in my brain. *What if he is dead? What if my dad is dead? Am I pushing hard enough? Is this working?*

1-2-3-4.

"Take over," I say to the useless woman standing behind me.

"What?" her eyes go wide and she shakes her head no.

"*Take over.* I'm getting tired."

"I don't know CPR," she stutters.

5-6-7-8.

A choked wail escapes me. I wipe my hand across my face full of snot and start again.

1-2-3-4.

"Come on. I need help. Please!"

Pinch nose. Two breaths.

I hear the toddler start wailing too. The fear is flowing off me. Consuming the room.

"Put your hands here." I show her. "Push as hard as you can."

5-6-7-8.

Pinch nose. Two breaths. I sit back on my heels. I swallow and start to plead. "Dad . . . Dad . . . Daddy . . . you have to wake up."

1-2-3-4.

I lean in and deliver two more breaths.

Sirens throb in the distance.

5-6-7-8.

The paramedics move me and take over. I go outside to the dirt patch yard.

1-2-3-4.

They work on him.

5-6-7-8.

They straddle over him as they bump him on the

stretcher across the barren yard into the ambulance. They press on.

1-2-3-4.

The ambulance twirls away. I am here. On the ground. I grab a patch of dirt. Clenching my hands in the scraggly grass. Maybe it will hold me. Maybe I am real. Maybe this is earth. But where? Here at a grungy house, in a terrible neighborhood, with strange people. *Who are these people? What happened to my dad?*

I am dazed. Shocked. *Am I awake?* One of the women tries to help me stand. I can't stand. I am broken. No. I shake loose and grip the grass. Shaking, rocking, repeating. I have to call my sister. I need my sister.

Somehow the phone is in my hand, and I call Ashlei. She cannot understand me. She tells me to call Mom. I don't want to. Mom will be mad at Dad. I call Mom. I need Mom. I need help. I need this grass. I need this earth to hold me.

The one woman tells me it happened to her dad too. *What happened to her dad? Too?! What has happened to MY DAD?*

I call Aunt Karen. I need a ride. I have to get away from here. *Where is here?* I don't know. I don't know. I don't know. A woman tells Karen an address.

They are talking to me. I cannot hear them. I cannot

hear. Shut up. Let me rock. Let me hold this earth. I want my dad. I want my mom. I want my sister.

The emergency room extends the nightmare. I rush to see my dad. To see him awake. He's not. His arms are flailing at the sides of the bed, his head rolling sideways, and a tube is in his throat. Why does he look like that? *Is he dead?*

The nurse pushes me to a police officer in the hall.

He says something.

"I don't know."

They sit me down.

Questions.

"No, I did not know where we were."

"No, I don't know who lives there."

"No, I do not know the women at the house."

"I don't know if I could identify them."
"I don't know."

"I am fifteen."

"No, I don't do drugs."

"No, I have never been there before. I don't live here."

"I live with my mom and stepdad in Illinois."

"I am here to visit my dad."

"Mom dropped me off this morning at my dad's house. We were going to a movie."

"*Jurassic Park III.*"

"I have never done drugs."

"No, I have not seen anyone do drugs."

"I don't know."

"I do not know why we were there."

"I don't know what happened."

"No, my dad does not do drugs. I don't think so. I don't know."

"No, I do not know where his phone is."

"He took a yellow pill before going into the house."

"I don't know where his wallet is."

"He was going to be five minutes."

"I had to pee."

"It was maybe thirty minutes. I don't know."

"I did not see anything. Not in the house. Not on the floor. Nothing."

"I don't know."

"Can I see him?"

"Is he okay?"

EACH STEP

Each step counted. Each day, week, month, and year counted. I had already been on the path, and it took self-sufficiency to walk me the rest of the way. It's a journey I am still on today. We all are.

Each month on my own, away from Matt, my self-worth grew. Each household job completed was a notch in my psyche. Each evening with happy, healthy children playing games and eating chicken and veggies was a win. Each step a victory. Those triumphs, large and small, built me up and confirmed I was not a loser. I was not a fat, stupid slob. I was a beautiful, healthy, active mom and career woman. I was strong and capable. I proved to myself with each step on my own. Each step lowered the pain in my and the girls' lives. Reducing the drama was powerful in creating stability and happiness for us.

When we moved to Northern Illinois, the drama plummeted in our lives. While we were living in Indiana, we were closer to the fluctuations of Matt's life. We were exposed to the variable nature of his visitation and whatever crisis Matt was experiencing, although we were not directly part of it. If he lost his job or did not have a car, we knew it and felt the impact from those events in our lives and community. If he had a trip to jail or his name was in the paper for being arrested, we felt the jolt of having to deal with it in some way. The spectacle was never-ending. After the move to Illinois, much of that went away for us because of the distance and network of friends. We did not know what was going on with him.

Matt's life continued its fits and starts. He was stuck in the same cycle he had been when I met him. But now I did not have to deal with it each day, each week, each month. Visitation became biannual, completely managed, scheduled, and executed by me. I maintained his visitations because that is what the research said was best. He could not get it together enough to coordinate a visit. The girls saw him after we moved because I made it happen. He never drove up, although he promised Olivia he would several times. The visitation defaulted to a summer and Thanksgiving stay. Each visit was fraught with worry for me. I fretted over leaving Olivia with him. *What if she were hurt? What if I never saw her again? What if she was forever marked, forever changed, by something that happened when she was with him?*

Matt's life ebbed and flowed. He charmed his way into someone's life, and they helped him out or took care of him for a few years. He rented a tiny house on the south side of town, then he lived in someone's guest house, then moved in and out of his mom's house, then he stayed with a couple in Winslow Farm, and then he moved in with a friend. His address was a revolving door. Matt worked, the same as he always had, sporadic and unreliable. The builders he worked for loved him for one, two, maybe three years, and then it unraveled and he'd look for a job again. I can assume his drug and alcohol use ebbed and flowed too. For the eleven years I was with him, he was never sober. Not one week, not one month. Sobriety was not part of who he was, at least not with me.

The women in his life also rotated through. There were girlfriends around. They did not last long. Sometimes it was helpful when he had a girlfriend because I could coordinate better with them instead of Matt. The pill-popping, drug-using girlfriends were not so helpful. I do not know how many of his girlfriends my girls met. Ashlei and Olivia had a different experience at my home. My mom had many men in and out of my life as a child, and I was committed to not doing the same. It was important to me the girls knew they were my priority, along with work. In the seven years I was single, they met two men, and the second one became my husband.

Ashlei grew into an active young lady, always one of the most popular girls in school. This brought with it a level of drama I was unaccustomed to. The popular crew had constant infighting and backstabbing. More than once, Ashlei had to seek out new friend groups because the girls were mean. She got decent grades. Her room was a mess. She was a feisty, emotional young teenager. Her wrath was not unfamiliar to me, and often reminded me of my sister Lori. Olivia and I did the same as Mom and I had done around Lori and tried to give Ashlei her space and avoided getting her angry.

Freshman year introduced Ash to Bloomington South, the same high school I had attended. Orientation was surreal, meeting my same teachers at that high school. Ashlei had the natural charm of her father, bouncy extroversion of her mother, and she remained steadfastly popular. We moved away halfway through her sophomore year, and I drastically underestimated what this meant for her. I took her away from everything she knew, and she was not going to forgive me. After three days at her new school, we decided it wasn't working, and we registered her to a private Catholic school for the final eight weeks of the school year. Although she became instantly popular at the new school too, it was an unmitigated disaster at home. Ashlei threatened to run away. She was going to get back to Bloomington, no matter what.

In order to prevent her from running off, I allowed her to go back. I worked with Matt and his mom, we built a plan, and she went back to Indiana to stay with her dad. She lived with him for six weeks. I have never been told what happened or how bad it was, but Ashlei's Aunt Karen contacted me. She was worried about Ashlei's safety. She simply told me, "It wasn't working." We agreed that Ash would move in with her. Karen and her husband were, and are, saints for taking Ashlei in and keeping her safe.

Ashlei came home to Northern Illinois for the summer and was at our house on her sixteenth birthday. She decided she wanted to move home with us. It was fantastic having her home. She was amazing. Since the decision was hers and it was not thrust on her, it was a positive move. She tried new activities, golf, track, and eventually made her way back to cheer. She had excellent junior and senior years in high school. She helped with the younger children, affection-ately referred to as the littles, and did everything we asked. Maybe she did not keep her room as clean as we liked; outside of that, her final years of high school were smooth.

Olivia's road was bumpy in different ways. Olivia was our baby, mine and Ashlei's. We protected her and kept her safe. We did not tell her or expose her to any of the pain and trauma Matt brought into our lives. The blue house in Bloomington had been endless joy for Olivia. She had a best friend next door and a safe neighborhood to explore where many of her other friends lived. She went to school with a teacher she loved. She was a happy, stable, dream-filled young girl.

We moved to Illinois when Olivia was in third grade. She too was taken away from everything and everyone she knew and loved. Then, after it being us three girls her whole life, Brad moved in and brought with him his young daughter. Then Brad and I had a baby shortly after we got married. Olivia is quiet, probably our most introverted child. She had to adjust from being the baby to being a big sister. She had to adjust from being the center of my attention to sharing me, with a man and two babies.

We all had to adjust. It was stable, happy, and predictable. We were safe. We were loved. There was no violence or drugs waiting to pounce on the home we created.

MATT'S EPILOGUE

Olivia was young-ish when we moved, and we sheltered her from the reality of Matt. She looked at Bloomington through rose-colored glasses and said everything was perfect there. She routinely threatened to move in with Matt after she became a teenager. Although it was an empty threat, it hurt, and she had no idea what her dad was really like because I had protected her from the truth.

The summer visitations kept up because I coordinated them. I drove Olivia to Indiana that fateful summer, and we had spent the weekend in Bloomington with family and friends. We went to all our favorite places, including getting ice cream at the Chocolate Moose and swimming in the quarry. It was a marvelous weekend.

When I dropped Olivia off to be with her dad, something was niggling at me. An unnamed dread. I did not know what was wrong, but I could tell something was off. Matt had broken up with someone and was moving back in with his mom again. He seemed vacant. I begged and pleaded with them both to delay the visit. I had to be in Indianapolis for work two weeks later, and I could bring Olivia down for a visit the subsequent week instead.

Olivia heard nothing of it. She was going to stay. She

was going to visit her dad, and I couldn't stand in her way. She was fifteen and adamant.

"Hope, we'll be fine," Matt said.

"Are you sure?"

"Yeah. I'm not going to let anything happen to her."

Before I left, I told Olivia, "You are responsible for your safety. Call me. Call your Aunt Karen. You stay safe." I paused for effect, and Olivia rolled her eyes. "If you get nervous, have any questions at all, get a quiver of being uncomfortable or unsafe or anything, anything at all, call Aunt Karen. Okay?"

"Mom," she groaned. "I'm going to be fine."

I gave Olivia a hard hug and reminded her once again to stay safe and that I loved her. She hugged me back and was ready to spend time with her dad.

"Are you okay?" I asked Matt.

"Yeah, Hope. I got this. We'll have a good time." He looped an arm around Olivia's shoulders. "I'm taking her to see *Jurassic Park* today."

"Okay, well, keep my baby safe, Matt." Tears threatened to spill.

The nights before any visits with Matt since we moved away were filled with dread. I feared for my girls' lives. I stayed up all night fretting. No matter. Matt had a legal right to see his children, and they wanted to. All the research said I should let their visits continue. I did not have any specific knowledge of current drug use; he had been out of our daily lives for many years. I had no idea what was going on with him. There was no real reason I could give for the worry. They always came home safe and happy, but I felt sick leaving them with him.

This time the dread felt different. I felt different. I wept as I drove away. I could not give specifics of what I feared. I was not concerned about Matt. I thought of Olivia and worried about harm that might befall her. I feared he might have a shady friend who would rape her, or crap, I don't know. I do not know what I feared. I was terrified for Olivia's safety when I dropped her off that morning. Something gnawed at me, and I was a wreck, hiccup-crying for forty-five minutes after dropping her off.

When I was an hour into the drive back home, I texted her and she responded everything was fine.

I drove on and was starting to relax. About the time I thought maybe I was worrying for no reason, I got a hysterical call from Olivia. She was bawling and told me they had taken her dad to the hospital in an ambulance. I told her to call Aunt Karen. I called Ashlei, took the next exit, looped around, and headed south.

I was three hours away from my baby, who was stuck in a nightmare. The drive back was three long hours of tears and fear.

Matt was forty-six, appeared to be in good health, and

they did not know how long he had gone without oxygen, so the ER doctors and nurses performed heroics to save him. There was no brain activity upon his arrival at the hospital, and they were unsure if it would return. They knew he had been administered CPR upon discovery. They eventually knew it was performed by his daughter.

The medical team lowered Matt's body temperature for two days attempting to reduce any swelling and to ensure no further brain damage occurred. The lines marched across the EEG with no movement. They then reheated his body to normal temperatures for twenty-four hours. The neurologist did a series of tests. The lines stayed flat.

Throughout those days, we all stayed at the hospital. Olivia took the afternoon and night shift, Ashlei took the day, and I spread myself in between. Olivia stayed all night with me and one of her cousins. I left around three or four in the morning, slept in the hotel for an hour or two, and returned with Ashlei at 7:00 a.m. Tom never left Ashlei's side. Brad, who had been in London, arrived and did the rounds with me.

We held Matt's hands. We talked to him. We also sat in silence. His mom, stepdad, sisters, brother, in-laws, nieces, nephews, aunts, uncles, and friends all came. My mom, sister, and friends came and brought food and stayed with us, keeping vigil in the waiting room.

The neurologist came for a final round of tests. It was

morning, Ashlei's shift. She was surrounded by me, Brad, and one of her aunts when the neurologist officially declared Matt brain-dead. The doctor said what we all knew. It did not make the hearing of the pronouncement any less hard.

Ashlei as next-of-kin had to make the hard decisions. Me, Brad, and the aunts were her "board of directors." None of us could make the final choices; Ashlei had to do it. And we knew telling Olivia would be devastating.

Together, Ashlei, Brad, and I told Olivia. She broke. She shrieked and folded. She died in front of my eyes. The room shrunk and she escaped, ran out screaming and wailing in a blur.

Olivia had found his body on the couch on Monday, he was declared dead on Thursday, and they wheeled him into final surgery for organ donation on Sunday. The entire family walked him, his body, to the OR doors. Ashlei made the right decision. The decision Matt wanted. The decision he signed for on his driver's license. Matt may have had his issues while living. Now he would give away his organs and tissues to help save and extend the lives of others.

My daughters' pain was inexplicable. Watching our girls suffer was beyond any of my own pain. Seeing them cry over Matt's bed and plead for his life was the worst. There is nothing I could do to ease their pain, release their sadness. Brad stood with us. Strong and sure. Supportive and full. Tom too.

Matt was not a traditional father figure and could not be counted on for "fatherly" things. He loved his girls; there is no doubt. I believe he would be angry with himself for how his death transpired—how it hurt his girls, how they had to experience it. No matter his faults, he loved them. And they love him.

Ashlei was twenty-one and Olivia was fifteen when they had to bury their dad. Ashlei has Matt's charm, and Olivia his optimism. They both have his zest for life. He faced many demons during his time on earth. He succumbed to a final bad choice. We held a small private service, and I wrote his obituary. Brad spoke at his funeral. Nothing could have been done without Matt's older sister, who is light unto this world.

They are loved, my girls, they are loved and cared for. This trauma, this pain, is unparalleled, indescribable. They made it through, will continue to make it through, and they live their lives as survivors. They must write the story of their own lives regardless of their father's life, death, or how it occurred.

We all must write our own story, no matter what circumstances we go through. Our past pain does not define us. How we choose to cope and thrive is what matters.

FLASH FORWARD: SNOW DAY

I sit on the couch, in our new rental house in our new state of Illinois. Taking the promotion was the right thing, I remind myself. Moving the girls is the right thing. We are going to be okay.

I like this place. The hardwood floors gleam, and the thrift store furniture is eclectic and fun. The couch, a 1970s green and yellow floral thing in mint condition, along with the yellow credenza with matching 1990s euro end tables are totally fabulous. The best piece is a white low-fat-square coffee table I decided on instead of a dining room table. I put pillows around the table, and people are to sit on the floor. This pièce de résistance sits on the marble floor of the sunken dining room and fits perfectly. Quirky. One of a kind. Perfect.

I swirl my coffee with Olivia nestled beside me. Eight inches of snow lie on the ground, and I announce there is no school today. She snuggles in the crook of my side and exhales a heavy sigh.

The move had been hard on all of us, so this restful time in the morning on a day home from school is welcome. We are still in our pajamas. She talks about the new friends she is making at school, and I listen as I stroke her hair. The snowplow rambles by disturbing the quiet.

"Do you want something special for breakfast? Pancakes?" I ask, as I lift myself off the deep comfy couch. Olivia lays her head on the pillow I had been leaning on.

"Sure."

"Just sure?"

"I don't know, Mom. Do we have bagels?"

Another loud engine heaves past the house. I glance out and see the school bus.

"Hey! Is that your bus?"

Olivia pops up and looks out the bay window.

"Yes!" She turns to me with panic. "Do we have school? I thought you said there was no school!"

"Well," I respond, in search of my phone, "I don't know. I assumed there was no school."

"What? You don't know?"

"Well, it snowed eight inches. Look at it out there!" I gesture to the window. "Who knew there could be school? Look at all the snow!"

If eight inches of snow dumped on us overnight in southern Indiana, there definitely would be no school. In Northern Illinois, it is just another day. I wrongly assumed the weather called for a snow day. The school district had not declared a day off. So I do. I do not scramble around and hurry to get us to school and work. I call us both in, and we take a respite day.

We need the time, Olivia and me. Ashlei is back in Bloomington. There has been so much to adjust to. First, Northern Illinois might as well be Siberia. Cold, windy, and grey. It had been grey for three straight weeks. My coworkers didn't bat an eye. I found it unnerving. *Where is the sun? OMG, what are we doing here? How do people survive here?*

We had lived in Bloomington, Indiana, our entire lives. And we had moved away from friends, family, schools, and a community that was small and easy to maneuver. Suburban life is different. And we do not know anyone here. I know people at work. We are not outside-of-work friendly yet.

The trip up here had been a challenge too. Olivia had ridden with Mom in the Camry while I drove the U-Haul in front of them, leading the way. Olivia had laid on the floor of the front seat with a blanket over her, blubbering the entire time. To say she did not want to move was an understatement.

Ashlei rode with me and she did not cry, but our anxiety was high. We pretended to pull it off and suck it up for the trip. Ashlei and I bumped along in the front seats of the big truck, talking about things that would change. The scope of change in this move was more massive than I could imagine, and I grossly underestimated what we were facing. *What have I done? What am I doing to my daughters? Is this a mistake?*

Somewhere deep inside of me, I knew I was doing the right thing. For my girls, for me, for all of us. We pulled up in front of the little rental house, and I felt a glimmer of excitement. I'd had the green and yellow floral couch sent up the week before. When we walked into the new place, our new home, a place I thought the girls would love, I was blindsided by the reaction.

Ashlei flipped. The house was horrible! The furniture was horrible! I was horrible! What was I doing moving them across country! How could I do this to us? Ashlei holding it together for the drive up fell apart the minute she stepped across the threshold of the house. I guess seeing the 1970s sofa was somehow the last straw. I half consoled her and half let her burn it off. We had to move through it. She had to process her turmoil, and I let her vent.

Mom and Olivia are not far behind. Their responses are less hysterical. Olivia probably has cried her tear ducts dry on the drive up. Instead we get to work. The four of us empty the big moving truck. Box after box after box. The TV is too heavy and awkward to carry, so we scoot it across the floor on a skateboard and pull it down the stairs on a blanket.

Thunk.

Thunk.

Thunk.

One step at a time.

That is how this move, and all of life, unfolds. One step at a time.

The snowplow makes another pass down our street. I look at my sweet daughter on the couch. "Yes, we have bagels. Come on. Let's eat."

She is making her way, we all are. One step at a time.

Epilogue

This book was hard for me to write. Much harder than the first book, *Hopey*. This may surprise some readers because the first book was intense too. With this one, I sobbed while writing some chapters and sections and memories. I cried so hard my glasses were flecked with tears, and I typed without them. I never cried while writing *Hopey*. There were pieces that made me anxious, nervous, or upset, but I did not openly cry. Writing this book has been an entirely different experience.

I'm not sure why. Maybe it's because the events in this book are more recent. I have had decades to process my childhood experiences, and this is my more recent past. Perhaps it's because I have not worked through these experiences. I don't know. As an adult, a single mom, I had to plow on. I could not be crippled by fear. I had to keep going. I had to take my steps to confidence, and I could not do that while lamenting the experiences themselves. I had to move forward. And I did.

Maybe it is because of my own culpability in the events. My own agency in the story. I feel guilty. I am guilty. I feel horrible for letting my girls see and hear the things they saw. I am devastated for being the mom that I was for the five months of addiction. I am culpable for the moments of terror they experienced, the abuse they witnessed and I stayed for. I allowed Matt to treat Ashlei bad enough that his friends were concerned. I own that. While I can tell myself I did my best, hindsight is twenty-twenty and I should have done something different, better, gotten out sooner. I know I did my level best. I am doing my best now. I am moving on. Moving forward.

The worst part? Even as I wrote this book, I questioned myself. Was it my fault? Maybe it wasn't so bad. Maybe it was me. Is this really abuse? Was I really being abused? If I could just do the cooking, cleaning, being, doing, communicating—all of it—better. Maybe I was the reason he was so angry all the time. I mean, is it too much to ask to fold the towel next to the sink? It does not seem too much to ask to put away dishes. See how insidious it is? The mindset, the belief, of the abused. All these years later, and I am still taking it on my shoulders; somehow it must have been my fault, and maybe it was not that bad. Intellectually I know better. I have read the articles. I know the data and the psychology of abuse. Even now I struggle to break free of the thinking. Thinking it is me, somehow my fault, and I was not good enough. Not good enough to be loved and appreciated for who I am. That it all was not too much to ask.

The second worst part? The list. I am now the keeper of the list. Matt ingrained in me certain habits and expectations. I don't like the sink to have anything in it. I like it dried out. This is crazy, I know. I enjoy the cans in the pantry facing the same direction. I prefer all closet and dresser drawers closed. I fold the towel and lay it next to the sink. The difference is, if they are not done, I don't get upset. I don't get mad. I either fix it or let it be however it is. These are a part of me, how I like my environment to look. As I age, my desire for order and neatness grows. He trained me. The list is my own now.

The third worst part is the reach for the "I feel so pink" is much further, so much harder. I do have unabashed happy moments, but they are fewer and farther between. This is probably normal. As your life experiences stack up, even reading the news buries our ability to reach joy without concern. The whisper of fear tickles my neck. I jump with each phone call. *Who is it? What is wrong? Is someone hurt?* An ambulance races by, and I am praying it is not one of my daughters in a wreck. I allowed Matt to shape my joy, shape my "pinkness." I allowed him to make fun of and steal my happiness. He belittled my pleasure and used it against me for eleven years. Don't let yourself be lost in the lens of someone else's eyes. Especially joy. Especially happiness. If you feel "pink," embrace it, relish it, and find a way to hold on to it so you can feel it more often.

This is my story. My girls have their own story to tell, all of them will. I have an incredible family, a successful career, and, importantly, a healthy marriage. I have a partner in this lifetime now. I make all decisions with him. We are connected, attached, and love each other in ways I did not know possible. Brad is not my savior; no one can save you. You have to save yourself. Brad is my partner, my lover, my best friend, my confidant, and the center of my being.

My girls are too. Children take a piece of your soul with them when they emerge. My belief is the entire process of parenting, after age six or seven, is about letting go. Letting them be themselves. I'm here for them, in every way possible, and I make every attempt to not project my desires and expectations onto them. I cannot experience their lives for them. I cannot take their pain for them either, even if I want to. I trust they are here to live their journey. They are my world. They have my heart. They are my heart.

Do I have any big life answers? I don't know. All I can do is take my own steps. I can continue on my march forward. I will continue to grow. To live. To experience joy and, yes, pain. I am not devoured or defined by my pain. My life is happy and fulfilled.

Is my life unusual or different? No. I am one of seven

billion souls here on earth. And I feel if I can tell my story, you might not feel so alone. Because you are not alone.

Whatever you are facing, you can persevere and over-come. You are stronger than you might think. You can make your life something you are proud of. You can feel safe. You can make yourself a home.

It is my sincere wish that in these pages, you find your own hope and it buoys and inspires you. I love hearing from my readers, and I thank you for taking this ride with me. Thank you for reading. Please reach out to me at hope@hopey.net.

Love,

Hope

Resources

National Resources for Sexual Assault Survivors and Their Loved Ones
1-800-656-HOPE
www.rainn.org

National Domestic Violence Hotline
1-800-799-7233
www.thehotline.org

Substance Abuse and Mental Health Services
1-800-662-HELP
www.samhsa.gov

National Drug and Alcohol Helpline
1-844-289-0877
www.drughelpline.org

Planned Parenthood
1-800-230-7526
www.plannedparenthood.org

Note: Neither the author nor the publisher are mental health professionals and do not make specific recommendations. This resources page is for informational purposes only as the reader deems useful. Always seek advice from a mental health professional to resolve problems or treat mental health issues.

POSTSCRIPT: TOO EASY?

As I reread this work, I wonder if I make it sound too easy—especially if you are in the middle of a divorce where abuse has occurred. It's not easy. My story here, this retelling, is a glancing blow, a bounce across the top of how hard it really is. I did not go in-depth in many areas. Perhaps it is because, as a coping mechanism, I put the trauma in a box and do not visit there often or because it is just too hard, too hard to describe, too hard to live through. Maybe it does not make for interesting reading. In order to address this "incompleteness," I include this postscript. The truth is, being in—and getting out of—an abusive relationship is nearly impossible. If I help one person face this challenge, it will be worth the share.

Where to begin?

Maybe it first begins with the decision to leave. Let me share some advice. Take what resonates.

The legal hurdles are real, so start with securing an attorney. I found an attorney through little research. I just picked one; I think I found him in the phone book. More research here is warranted and should be easier with the proliferation of the internet. Ask trusted friends for references. There, of course, is the expense. My retainer fee then was $500, and it was not easy to come by. Retainer fees for a decent attorney are probably much more now. I recommend shopping for the right attorney before agreeing to work with one. Meet with him or her. Confirm they are aligned and supportive with what you want to do and are someone you can trust.

My attorney was not great. He was looking towards his own retirement, and I don't think he cared to fight for what was best for me. He wanted a quick win and closure off his plate. He pushed hard for joint custody, with my having primary physical custody, simply because it would be easier to resolve and get through the courts. Decide what you want to do and your parameters before speaking with an attorney. Make a list of your goals and determine whether the lawyer will support those requirements. Also decide on which things you are willing to compromise. I did not have to do much compromising on financial issues because we had the prenuptial agreement. The prenup outlined the division of our assets. After discussions with the attorney, decide if you are willing to do what it takes to get what you want. If you are financially limited and in an abusive situation, you may start with an abuse shelter. They have a full complement of services and are able to guide you through a difficult process, supporting you legally, financially, and emotionally.

Was leaving Matt easy? No. I had to get a restraining order against him. After he moved out, he broke into our home a few times and destroyed my belongings. He threatened me with anything you could think of, and I did not feel safe. Because he got into the house, the police were involved, they took pictures, and filed a report. It all was ammunition against him.

In order to get a restraining order, you need enough courage, and money, to request the courts for the order. Attorneys are involved, the court is involved. Then you, the one who is being threatened daily, must go to court and prove why you feel unsafe. The tears and stress during this time are unlimited. The court was unfeeling. The opposing attorney may try to belittle the reality the abused person is facing. The onus is on the victim to prove that she/he is being abused and are concerned for their safety and the safety of their children. In my story, the restraining order was granted to protect me. They did not find enough evidence to limit Matt's access to the children, thus making the restraining order effectively null because I had to do childcare exchange with him. Ridiculous, I know. I do hope things have improved in the court system now. In some states and counties, I know things are handled differently. This was the situation in Indiana in the early 2000s.

A restraining order is an ineffective means to prevent full access to the victim. You are armed with a piece of paper. In the event the abuser comes near, your recourse is to call the police each time the abuser violates the order. The entire premise of the restraining order is reactive and not preventative. My home was broken into and violated. I was threatened. I was lucky because Matt was not motivated to really hurt me and was not seeing the girls much then anyway.

Even though the system is flawed, a restraining order is still a powerful tool. It may be difficult to obtain and near impossible to enforce, yet it is good to have. Each legal exchange, each police visit, each public record of behavior and abuse establishes a picture of the abuser. The restraining order is documented evidence of the abuse and events that occurred at home, in private. It makes the threats objective evidence and becomes a legal document establishing the behavior of the abuser. If you fear for your safety or the safety of your children, discuss it with your attorney. If you feel strongly about it, get a restraining order.

Take care of yourself and ensure the safety of your children. Each of these actions is a claw back. Establish yourself as a human being who deserves love, respect, and care. Abuse is not acceptable, and taking back your life is important. Every effort you make grows your strength and confidence.

I also touched on, but largely skipped over, the financial strain of divorce. I was not too financially strapped because I had a good job and a growing career. Yet I incorrectly believed the divorce papers protected me from Matt's debts and financial commitments. There were real financial blows that took years to resolve, and my divorce was the most expensive thing I have ever undertaken. And it was worth every penny.

Matt and I had a prenuptial agreement, which Matt's mom had insisted we sign. At the time I was appalled and embarrassed. I get it though. I was on the tail end of my drug addiction, and I came from an underprivileged family. She wanted to protect her son. At the time we decided to marry, Matt had a running lie that he had won $10,000 in the lottery. It was absurd, and I did not believe it, and I didn't think Matt had money. However, his mom believed this running lie, and she did not want me to take advantage of her son. The prenup was penned and signed prior to our wedding, and, in the end, the agreement protected me.

The prenup stated anything individually generated throughout the marriage was property of the sole named owner—which meant he had no access, or future access, to my growing retirement account, stocks, and other real monies I had been issued from my jobs at Eli Lilly and Cook or the condo. These were all in my name only. Matt's credit was so bad, so it was cleaner to not have him on the mortgage. The prenup left little negotiating room for Matt because he had already agreed to the parameters before our marriage. The prenup was a huge blessing, but I still got stuck with his debt.

During our marriage, I was the person who took care of and paid all of the bills each month. Matt was terrible with money. Our divorce decree stated he was to pay for his Jeep Wrangler. I was responsible for the Toyota Camry. I was able to keep the Camry no matter what because it was solely in my name. I had cosigned the Jeep with him because he could not get financing on his own. After the divorce, no surprise, he did not make his payments for the Jeep. He did work and clearly had cash for drugs, booze, and women. Creditors called the house all the time. I was the one responding. Silly me, I shared the divorce decree with the creditors thinking they would leave me alone. They called constantly and wrote nasty letters.

The creditors threatened to repossess the Jeep. Finally, one day in a fit of frustration, I told them Matt's address, thinking the repossession would resolve the debt. After they took it early one morning Matt called in a rage and accused me of telling them where he lived. I said they must have figured it out some other way. I never admitted to Matt that I gave them his address so they could take the Jeep.

Repossession does not resolve the debt. The company repossesses the vehicle then sells it at auction. Rarely do they make at auction what is owed on the vehicle. Then the original debt holder, Matt and I in this case, is responsible for the difference between what was owed and what they got at auction. So the debt collector calls resumed. Who knew paying off $17,000 would be such a high mountain to climb?

These calls and letters are awful, a constant mental beat down. I foolishly thought a piece of paper from divorce court would keep me out of it. I thought I could handle the collectors. In hindsight, I should not have cosigned for him, even though we were married. Matt was never a good negotiator, and he got taken on the price of the car. I did not help him when he was buying it, just showed up to sign the paperwork, nothing else. It was stupid. I should not have done it—though it was easier than fighting about it, or worse.

The continuing calls from the debt collection agency escalated to court hearings. Matt never responded. He never went to court. I did. I took my trusty divorce decree with me to show them I was not liable. I talked about the restraining order, and the fact that we had been divorced and he had not made a single child support payment. Not one. The people in court seemed to sympathize but the law was unyielding. The attorney for the financing company, the judge, and the bailiff all empathized. The bailiff kept bringing me tissues. The judge still found me liable. Why? Because I was there.

I had been responding and corresponding with the debt collector throughout the period, even though it was to deny responsibility. I was also working at a job they could track. They did not even know Matt's address or phone number, and it did not matter if I gave it to them, which I had already done. He did not respond, ever. He never picked up a certified letter. He was not working somewhere with a normal W-2 or where his income could be tracked.

The good citizen that I was, I showed up. I corresponded, thinking the decree protected me from having to pay. Then I banked on the goodness of humans. They felt bad. The law was clear and not in my favor. They found me, and Matt, liable for the debt. Since I was the one there, and the one with trackable income, I was the one who paid. They garnished my wages at the hearing. It was embarrassing. The court contacted my employer and coordinated the garnishment of wages, a rate that would take years to pay off the total debt. I paid off the remaining balance when I sold the condo and made a little money. Not a lot, but a little, and I used it to pay off a Jeep I never drove, never had, and was not responsible for. I had to put an end to the wage garnishment for my mental health.

Through the curtain of tears and snot sobs, the judge admonished me and encouraged me. She said she hated to find me liable and instructed me to immediately go to the family services office and submit the paperwork for his failure to pay child support. I did. I did it that day. I entered the paperwork for them to prosecute Matt for failure to pay child support.

Matt was furious. How could I do that to him? Now they chased him for child support. The process got the courts, prosecutor, and purportedly the sheriff involved. Matt should not have been upset, and I should not have bothered. He never paid a dime through the court. Not one dime.

Matt died with over $50,000 in arrears. He never paid. No one ever made him pay child support. He never, not once, had any consequences for not paying child support, other than the court dates he would periodically show up to asking for a delay. This went on until the day he died. We got divorced in 2002, Matt died in 2015, and he never paid. Never. Nothing. Nothing happened. The courts did not help. Plan to do it on your own. And if money shows up, it is a bonus to be deposited into your children's savings.

After the original divorce hearing where my tottering old attorney missed every beat and I scribbled him instructions on the yellow legal pad to make sure our points were made, I represented myself. I am not recommending this for everyone. It worked for me. It saved me attorney's fees, and with the internet and decent research, the courts and legal documents are simple to draft and submit.

Visitation scheduling was another significant hurdle.

Matt did not follow any schedule for nearly three years after the divorce. I remained flexible with his visitation. He did not take the girls much and typically saw them for a few hours here and there, mostly on what would have been his weekend. When he did start taking them on his scheduled weekends, it was an adjustment for all of us. When the girls came back on Sunday, it was an emotional transition day. He managed his home much differently. He ate and fed them unhealthily. One time Olivia happily reported she ate six corndogs for breakfast. At Matt's house, they watched unlimited TV. The list goes on. Suffice to say my home was the safe, routine, and consistent home, and Matt's was a wild card.

Matt's routine visitation petered out after about two years, and we were back to ad hoc visitation. I also finally stopped making excuses for him if he did not show up. All I wanted was to protect my girls from pain. In retrospect, I wonder about the core decision of maintaining Matt in their lives. All of the data at the time, and still today, shows that some level of contact and parental engagement is best for the children. Even with what went on in our house, Matt never laid a hand on the girls, and I could not have refused all visitation.

Ashlei was old enough to know Matt was a mess. She had been in the house during the demise, and his inconsistent presence and lack of integrity angered her. It is also likely that during his time with them, he was doing drugs and drinking with them around. She knew. Ashlei knew he was an addict. Olivia did not. Ashlei and I did all we could to protect Olivia. Whether we were right or not, we shielded her. Olivia did not know anything about his drug use. One of the first texts she sent Ashlei after she found Matt's body was: "Does Dad do drugs?" Mostly because she was questioned by the police. We had moved away when she was eight, and she did not spend much time with Matt; maybe he was on good behavior when they did have a visit once a year. Maybe we protected Olivia too much. I never told them, either Ashlei or Olivia, about all that happened with Matt and me. They don't know this story. Ashlei knew and saw much of it, but I do not know what she remembers—or how she remembers it.

The divorce decree did not protect them from being exposed to Matt's habits. The papers did include language that stated he could not drink to excess or do drugs prior to or during their visit. Again, this was impossible to enforce.

I do not know what is right. I do know Matt loved the girls and they loved him. I do not know how their mental health and their lives would have been different (or better) if they did not have contact with him.

My advice now is regardless of what the research says, define what you want, do your own research, and do what is best for you and your children. Make sure you can look back and know you did your level best to protect and raise them.

So, again, was any of this easy? Hell no. There are legal and financial burdens. What can I say about what it took emotionally? There is stress. Stress of the courts, attorneys, and hearings. Stress and fear of potential outcomes. Fear for my kids. Will they be hurt? Will they come home to me whole? These thoughts weighed on me, constantly.

Please, hear me. There is a better life on the other side of these hurdles. Stay the course, put the fear in a box, and do not let it guide your decision-making.

Fear will keep you down if you let it control you. You can use it as fuel to propel you to a new life. Your safety and a better life await. Your circumstances are yours alone. Know you can build a plan to make it. You can. Stay the course. Get help. Trust and believe you can get to the other side.

My life now is amazing. I could not imagine a life as good as I have today. Believe me, you can do it. It's not easy, but it is worth it. Go make your life amazing.

POST-POSTSCRIPT: DECISIONS

Through the launch of my first book, *Hopey: From Commune to Corner Office,* I had many interviews and many Q&A sessions at book signings. A lot of people asked me questions about regrets and decision-making. One person posed the query: "If I could change one thing, one decision, what would I tell my fifteen-year-old self?" These are hard questions for me—wondering about regrets or do-overs—because I do not live my life facing backward. I charge forward with abandon and push past fear. Have I made mistakes and bad choices? Absolutely. Beating myself up over them forever or wishing the past could be different is pointless.

If you have read both of my books, you know many of my choices were not necessarily the most well-thought-out. Some were not active decisions; they were default decisions. I realize there are decisions I recorded in these books that may make some people uncomfortable, or even angry. As

I got older, wiser, and more experienced, I became clearer about a decision-making framework, and there are three critical components I adhere to now.

#1 Be conscientious.

Take the bull by the horns and face your decisions directly. Do not pretend you do not have to decide—which is, itself, making a choice. Face up to whatever decision is before you, no matter how difficult it may seem. Avoidance usually is not the best route to achieving your desired outcomes.

Take all current variables into account. Talk to trusted partners and confidants about the options. Get all the information inputs needed to help make the decision. With mindful consideration, whatever the final decision is, you will believe in it and know the right decision was made at the time. If you are not thorough and specific in your decision-making, you instead live by default, and a lack of action could have a series of consequences. If it all goes sideways and the worst possible outcome occurs, you do not want to look back and regret the decision you made or your lack of process regarding it. You don't want to lie awake at night and think, *I should have done X! Why didn't I make an active decision? Why didn't I take an active direction?*

#2 Get help if needed.

If you have a life partner, make the decision with them. If you don't, build a network of supporters who can help you. They cannot make the decision for you. They can help you see alternatives and possible outcomes. If the decision is big enough, or complicated, get outside help as needed. Be wise in who you use for advice. Each family member in your life, outside of your partner, has their own agenda for your life and potentially your kids' lives. They have their own thoughts, own perceptions, own opinions of what your life should be. Even if they are well-intentioned and want the best for you, their ideas may not be fully aligned with how you feel. You are using them for guidance, not for final say-so. They do not have all of the facts, and all the feelings—only you do.

No one can make your decisions for you. No one has your set of experiences or has your knowledge. Often the best help to seek out is a therapist or social worker. They are neutral and can see the bigger picture without the bonds of family ties. A good therapist helps you sort out your thoughts and does little to guide or instruct you on what you should do. Take the time to find the right therapist if needed. Shop for them and treat the first session as an interview. This person helps usher you through your own processes and thoughts, so find someone who is the right fit. There are many wonderful therapists and counselors, so do not despair if you don't click with the first one you visit.

3 Do not make decisions out of fear.

This factor is the most important. Fear is a debilitating emotion and is not a good partner for good decision-making. Do not ignore real scenarios of danger, of course, but this discussion is not about your safety. This is about having the capability to make a tough decision, the decision you know is right. Fearful decision-making may have led me to stay with Matt even longer. It may have been "easier," and I could be dead today, just a few seconds away from blackness, if I had stayed any longer. Factually, getting out of an abusive relationship is what is best, even if it's hard or scary.

Push yourself outside of your comfort zone and know the good stuff is on the other side of fear.

Fear comes in all shapes and forms. When I bought the blue house and rented out the condo, my mom and a close friend were scared for me. *What are you going to do if the HVAC gives out? If you have to replace the refrigerator? If you have to do repairs to the condo? How are you going to afford it if you cannot get the unit rented?*

Do not ignore these people's input because those are potential outcomes and it's wise to consider various possibilities, but fear cannot be the basis of a final decision. This is why #2 above is to seek help. Make sure your final decision is yours and aligned with your goals and desires. Others can help you see things you may not have considered. In the end, your decision is yours.

No disaster befell me during the time I had both properties. I did not make a monthly profit. I broke even on the condo with the rent I collected. I was able to keep it rented, and I had renters lined up before I bought the blue house.

There have been many decisions that shaped my life. An obvious one was the decision to stop doing drugs. I stripped it down to the simplest components: good versus evil, drugs or Ashlei. Making the decision in this way simplified what the real choices were. I couldn't knowingly, consciously, mindfully, choose drugs over my daughter. For someone else choosing to stop drugs, their decision process may include checking into rehab or going to recovery meetings.

We all have had to make loads of decisions in life, and the goal is to make the fewest that might lead to regret.

Another hot button for some readers is the abortion. It was my conscientious decision. When I was pregnant with Ashlei, the decision was to continue the pregnancy. That is a choice I have made again, two more times. And the one time, I made a different choice. I have never lamented getting an abortion. I have never once thought about how old that child might be or what their life might look like. Firstly, because it was not a child, not yet. It was nonviable, same as a zygote in a cryo-chamber in an IVF clinic; there was not a viable child in my body. Secondly, I was not well. I was in the throes of drug addiction. I had probably already irrevocably damaged the blastocyst with the drug use. I was not stable with Matt. He was moving in and out of the apartment, and our life was filled with violence and pain. I had already shipped Ashlei off to her grandmother's during this period, and this was not a life for a child. This was not a life. This was not fair to any being. It was not right to bring another addicted young human into this set of experiences and environment. I don't regret the decision. I know without a doubt I made the best decision at the time with the information I had.

I have made the clear decision to share my private personal life on the pages of my books. I have seen from my first book that sharing these most vulnerable times has helped people, especially women. I imagine and am hopeful the content in this book can do the same. When I am asked now about my regrets, I simply say I cannot go back. I now make my decisions using these three guideposts.

I do want to encourage you to push past fears. When you are able to face your decisions honestly, you stretch yourself. This is where you grow. This is where life begins anew.

Whatever it is you are facing, know you have the power within you to make good decisions. Decide conscientiously, with trusted advisors, and without fear. You will be amazed at what your life can become.

BOOK CLUB
DISCUSSION GUIDE

The facilitators of the book discussion should be planful in their approach to discussing this book. The author shares traumatic stories, but book club members may or may not want to share theirs. If they decide to share their own stories, the club can expect an emotional discussion.* We suggest starting with that question.

1) Do we want to share personal stories or not as a group?

After that is established, the leader needs to actively guide the discussion away from topics they'd rather not share.

If participants decide to share, then trust rules must be established. The leader should be ready with tissues. If the group decides to share and tackle some of those areas, the group will know, trust, and appreciate each other in a deeper more profound way.

2) Did you like the book? What did you like about the book?

3) What aspects of the author's story could you most relate to?

4) What would you do differently in the author's position?

5) Why do you think Hope stayed with Matt so long?

6) If you read *Hopey: From Commune to Corner Office*, how did Hope's childhood shape these young adult decisions?

7) How do you think drug use and drug addiction impacted Hope's life?

8) How can we help victims of abuse break the cycle and safely change their lives?

9) Do you know, or have you known, victims of abuse? How are these reported and shared?

10) How can we maintain love and acceptance at our core through hardships?

11) What inspires you most about the story?

12) What other books did this remind you of?

13) How should victims discuss their experiences?

14) How do we positively impact the world around us to reduce these events?

15) How can we raise our children to be considerate and conscious of their own bodily autonomy and their friends' bodily autonomy?

16) How can we raise our children to avoid drugs and drug use?

Remember, you are valid. You are real. Your experiences are your own and shape who you are. You are amazing, powerful, and capable. Be you. Be amazing.

*Neither the author nor the publisher are mental health professionals and do not prescribe mental health practices or treatments. Always seek advice from a mental health professional to resolve problems or treat mental health issues.

ACKNOWLEDGMENTS

Here I am again, sitting down to write a thank you to all of the people who have helped and supported me through this feat of authoring a book. I am plagued with the same sensation that I will forget someone critical.

I thank Ashlei and Olivia. Much of this work is their story too and I thank them for letting me share it. I thank Brooke and Lauren for giving me time and privacy to get the work completed. I thank Brad Mueller, whose love and support has buoyed me throughout this process, and without whom this work would never have gotten finished, published, or marketed.

My editing, publishing, and marketing crew use a mix of encouragement, accountability and crisp honesty that keeps me going; Kelly Epperson, Beth Lottig, and Tiffany Harelik are indispensable in my writing life.

Thank you, Joyce Finn and the Writers and Critters group of international women. The submissions, critiques, wisdom, and unflinching support is powerful and deeply appreciated.

Beta-readers Jennifer Hottell, Jane Banning, and Meredith Merson's initial insight and feedback were essential for improving the work. I appreciate the time and commitment they so easily granted me.

My self-defined, voluntary marketing team: Susan Chambers (and her whole family), Katy Zabriskie, Jennifer Hottell, Jane Banning, Audra Coleman, Harry Jeffries, Dan Larrimore, Jennifer Bushey, Kristie Scott, Taylor Dukes, Katy Dukes, Holly White, Meredith Merson, Brad Mueller, Jennifer Harp, and Tiffany Harelik were my most treasured cheerleaders and helped shape the cover, back flap language, and never fail to provide opinions and guidance.

Thank you, Northwestern Executive MBA Cohort 122, and especially to my team: Prima Sengales, Akshay Arora, David Martinez, Chris Palmer, Rob Watson, and Alex Weishaar were supportive, interested, and helped with final cover decisions.

My employers continue to be happy supporters and I must thank Melanie Gloria, Michael DesJardin, Barry Moze, Matt Flesh, Kelly Jansen, Geoff Curtis, and Irina Konstantinovsky. Thank you, Chris Murphy, for the test drive.

Thank you, mom, for your unconditional love and encouragement of me, my writing, and most importantly Ashlei and Olivia. Thank you for all of the childcare hours,

I will never be able to repay you. Thank you for framing my degree.

Thank you to Matt's mom and sisters (and their husbands) for their love, wisdom, and guidance they shared with Ashlei and Olivia along the way. You were always there for them, especially in their darkest hours and the times they needed you most. Thank you to Mike Fidler for the conversation in the garage. Thank you for letting me know I did not have to live in fear and violence and that I, and the girls, deserved better.

A second thank you to Ashlei, Olivia, and Brad barely covers the million times I need to express this appreciation to you three.

Thank you, Jamaica White, for the conversation that saved my life and saved the lives of my daughters. Without you none of the rest of my life is possible. Thank you to the drug counselor for helping me hold myself accountable each day to the decision I made.

Finally, thank you to the young lady from class who joined me in the waiting room at Planned Parenthood. I was not alone that day because you showed up and cried with me. We can all be this mysterious woman. We can be a human who loves, cares, and supports others in the deepest time of need.

ABOUT THE AUTHOR

Hope Mueller is an author, inspirational speaker, and a results-driven leader who enjoys heading organizations, improving system performance, and launching efficient programs. She is a busy executive, sits on multiple not-for-profit boards, and has launched a local scholarship fund. She is also the chairman and president of a charitable organization that helps children and their families during critical junctures of their lives, Hunter Street Charities. To learn more please visit www.hunterstreetcharities.net; 10 percent of all proceeds from *Counting Hope* and *Hopey* will be donated to this charity.

Hope's passionate about promoting and developing leaders and in-need community support and investment. Hope's strength is the ability to create order out of chaos. She is a change agent with excellent strategic vision, tactical execution, communication and organizational capabilities. She has the rare ability to turn vision into reality.

Hope has a number of technical publishing credits on

a national level, is an international speaker and she authors business articles focusing on career development and positive managing up techniques. Hope's debut inspirational memoir was launched in October 2019.

Hope lives in northern Illinois, with her husband and actively parents her four daughters and grandson.

You may connect with Hope on these platforms:

Email: hope@hopey.net
Website: www.hopey.net
Facebook: HopeMuellerAuthor
Twitter: @hpmueller242
Instagram: hpmueller242
Goodreads: Hope Mueller